every woman's battle

promise book

**God's Words of Encouragement
to Guard Your Heart, Mind, and Body**

every woman's battle
promise book

foreword by Stephen Arterburn

Shannon Ethridge

WATERBROOK
PRESS

EVERY WOMAN'S BATTLE PROMISE BOOK
PUBLISHED BY WATERBROOK PRESS
12265 Oracle Blvd., Suite 200
Colorado Springs, Colorado 80921
A division of Random House, Inc.

All Scripture quotations, unless otherwise indicated, are taken from the *Holy Bible, New International Version®*. NIV®. Copyright © 1973, 1978, 1984 by International Bible Society. Used by permission of Zondervan Publishing House. All rights reserved. Scripture quotations marked (MSG) are taken from *The Message.* Copyright © 1993, 1994, 1995, 1996, 2000, 2001, 2002. Used by permission of NavPress Publishing Group. Scripture quotations marked (NKJV) are taken from the *New King James Version.* Copyright © 1982 by Thomas Nelson, Inc. Used by permission. All rights reserved. Scripture quotations marked (NLT) are taken from the *Holy Bible, New Living Translation,* copyright © 1996. Used by permission of Tyndale House Publishers, Inc., Wheaton, Illinois 60189. All rights reserved. Scripture quotations marked (RSV) are taken from the *Revised Standard Version of the Bible,* copyright © 1946, 1952, and 1971 by the Division of Christian Education of the National Council of the Churches of Christ in the USA. Used by permission. Scripture quotations marked (TLB) are taken from *The Living Bible* copyright © 1971. Used by permission of Tyndale House Publishers, Inc., Wheaton, Illinois 60189. All rights reserved.

ISBN 1-4000-7004-X

Library of Congress Cataloging-in-Publication Data
Ethridge, Shannon.
        Every woman's battle promise book : God's words of encouragement to guard your heart, mind, and body / Shannon Ethridge ; foreword by Stephen Arterburn.— 1st ed.
            p. cm.
        ISBN 1-4000-7004-X
    1. Christian women—Prayer-books and devotions—English. 2. Chastity—Prayer-books and devotions—English. 3. Love—Prayer-books and devotions—English. 4. Sex—Prayer-books and devotions—English. I. Ethridge, Shannon. Every woman's battle. II. Title.
    BV4844.E84 2005
    241'.66—dc22   2004021649

Printed in China
2006

10 9 8 7 6 5 4

contents

foreword

(by Stephen Arterburn)

Many confusing and conflicting voices come at us from all directions through the Internet, television, movies, billboards, and reading material. These voices can make us wonder what is right, what is good, and what is the next best thing to do. We don't need more voices that confuse us and lead us down paths we were never meant to travel. Thankfully there is one source that heals and soothes and encourages us. In the midst of the noise and confusion, it comforts me to know that God's Word is always there, always providing truth, wisdom, and hope. It never fails, always delivering on its promises.

Sadly, not everyone sees the Bible as a source of comfort. Some people have been brought up to focus on only one aspect of God's Word. They have been taught the dos and the don'ts, and they have been warned of the consequences of disobedience. Most everything they have heard from Scripture has been negative and restraining. Does this sound familiar? Do you see the Bible as a tool that has been used against you rather than a source of strength and a guide toward the most amazing life you could possibly live? If so, I hope this little book changes that for you.

John 10:10 is one of the greatest promises in Scripture. If we believe what it says, it will cause us to search God's Word for more of what God has to offer. It reads, "The thief's purpose is to steal and kill and destroy. My purpose is to give life in all its fullness" (NLT). I have found this to be absolutely true. The thief, or Satan, has tempted me with many things I thought were good, but they stole my joy, killed my hope, and destroyed my peace. It was only when I turned my life completely over to God that I found life that was abundant and full.

This powerful message, this promise of a great life, is just one of the powerful and positive promises God offers us. Most of us just don't spend enough time focusing on those promises and living to see them fulfilled in our lives. This book is a tool to do just that. We hope that no matter what else you do in your personal Bible study, you will begin to spend a little time every day focusing on God's promises to you. This little book is designed to make that easy to do. We believe that when you fill your heart and mind and soul with these promises, the rest of life is much easier to bear. We think God's promises will motivate you to live your best life and will be a great encouragement to you as you walk with Him and live for Him.

every woman's battle
promise book

introduction

You may be wondering why you need *Every Woman's Battle Promise Book.* Perhaps you've read *Every Woman's Battle,* and you more than likely own a Bible or at least have access to one. In answer to your question, I'd like to tell you what inspired me to create this special little book you are holding in your hands.

I have been overjoyed at the numerous e-mails and letters received in response to *Every Woman's Battle.* The vast majority of these praise reports speak of changed lives, strengthened marriages, and renewed spirits. However, one recurring comment has concerned me: "I have made *Every Woman's Battle* my daily devotional book."

While I was happy to know I had touched on a topic so near and dear to women's hearts that they would turn to our book every day for a season of their lives, I was also disconcerted. As more women verbalized this decision, I worried that if they were going to turn to only one book on a daily basis, it needed to be God's Book, not ours.

I've read many powerful, inspiring books on the topic of sexual temptation and emotional fulfillment. They have ranged in focus from how to break relationship addictions to why women love until it hurts to how to have a more godly marriage. These books have been great resources, and God has certainly used them in my life, but none of them had the power to truly make a lasting difference. They may have changed how I saw my situation, but I continued to see myself, my marriage, and God through my own narrow view. Only one Book took off my blinders and helped me understand the fullness of who I truly am in Christ, what God had already done for me to set me free, and the rich rewards that He has in store for me as I choose to walk in obedience. That Book, of course, is the Bible, written by God Himself.

Josh McDowell eloquently coined the phrase, "Rules without relationship lead to rebellion."[1] Prior to my diving into God's Word, I knew the rules well—do not commit adultery, abandon lustful desires, avoid even a hint of sexual immorality—but because my relationship with God had no depth, rebellion continually welled up inside me. Oh, I had gone to church my entire life, sung hymns, and was the president of my youth group. I could recite John 3:16 and Psalm 23. But how could I have thought that I had a genuine relationship with God when His personal love letter to me sat on my shelf, collecting dust from day to day?

About four years into my marriage, I realized that my wandering heart could very well destroy our young family. My personal battle for sexual and emotional integrity grew so fierce that out of desperation, I began dusting that Bible off and searching, sometimes begging, for a word from God to help me hold on just

---

1. Josh McDowell, *The Disconnected Generation* (Nashville, TN: Word, 2000), 28.

one more day. I felt I had no one to confide in about my secret struggles, but one day I sensed God beckoning me into His Word. There I discovered two scriptures that God gave directly to me in response to my cries for help:

No temptation has seized you except what is common to man. And God is faithful; he will not let you be tempted beyond what you can bear. But when you are tempted, he will also provide a way out so that you can stand up under it.

1 CORINTHIANS 10:13

For we do not have a high priest who is unable to sympathize with our weaknesses, but we have one who has been tempted in every way, just as we are—yet was without sin. Let us then approach the throne of grace with confidence, so that we may receive mercy and find grace to help us in our time of need.

HEBREWS 4:15-16

As I read these verses I couldn't help but think, *You mean I'm not the only one who struggles with this, God? You really understand what it's like to be tempted? You mean you're going to show me how to get out of this relational mess before I ruin everything?* These revelations shed new light on my situation, and they also gave new life to my self-esteem and my relationship with Jesus Christ. I couldn't fathom that His love for me was so unconditional and that He could muster so much compassion, even after I'd been so rebellious. But I had to believe it because God Himself said it. It wasn't something that a contemporary author had written without any personal knowledge of me or my situation. It was something that God had written to me long ago, before I even came into existence, and He was fully aware of the compromising situation that I'd be in when I would finally stumble upon these precious words of His.

I began responding to His lavish love and continued to dig deeper and deeper into the Bible for more life-sustaining encouragement. I soon found myself longing to have an obedient spirit. Oh, how I wanted to honor God with my every thought, word, and deed! I desired desperately to become the woman He created me to be and to serve Him consistently. When I read Psalm 51, I felt an immediate connection with David and suspected that I was, in fact, slowly becoming a woman after God's own heart:

Create in me a pure heart, O God,
  and renew a steadfast spirit within me.
Do not cast me from your presence
  or take your Holy Spirit from me.
Restore to me the joy of your salvation
  and grant me a willing spirit, to sustain me.
Then I will teach transgressors your ways,
  and sinners will turn back to you.

PSALM 51:10-13

Many months later, I sensed God's prompting to begin writing and ministering to other women who, like me, had looked for love in all the wrong places. I had discovered Living Water and it tasted too good not to share it with other thirsty women! However, the thought of making my sexual struggles public information made me uncomfortable. I wasn't sure I could be so vulnerable about such an intimate topic and was especially fearful of how my family would respond. I begged God for confirmation that He would, in fact, give me the grace and confidence I needed to fulfill such a calling and asked for reassurance that my family could somehow love me unconditionally as well. Then I came across Psalm 45, and it was as if God was painting a magnificent portrait of my life's mission statement:

My heart is stirred by a noble theme
      as I recite my verses for the king;
      my tongue is the pen of a skillful writer....
Listen, O daughter, consider and give ear:
      Forget your people and your father's house.
The king is enthralled by your beauty;
      honor him, for he is your lord....
All glorious is the princess within her chamber;
      her gown is interwoven with gold.
In embroidered garments she is led to the king;
      her virgin companions follow her and are brought
        to you.

They are led in with joy and gladness;

    they enter the palace of the king.

PSALM 45:1,10-11,13-15

These words gave me the vision that I needed and got my engine revved up! I believe ushering women into the presence of our King is exactly what I was *made* to do and nothing makes my heart sing like serving the Lord in this way. But I confess as an author, wife, and mother there are many days when I get tired of writing and doing things for others. I am sometimes tempted to fall back into old relational patterns of fantasizing about a man or getting my ego stroked by the handsome stranger sitting next to me on the airplane. That's when I reach into my mental Rolodex and bring out this scripture to meditate on:

To [her] who overcomes, I will give the right to sit with me on my throne, just as I overcame and sat down with my Father on his throne.

REVELATION 3:21

God's Word is living and active! It can do surgery on your heart and mind, girlfriend! His words can save your life, your marriage, and your sanity. His affirmations can lead you toward a comfort, peace, joy, and hope that you could never know outside of an intimate connection with the Author. But you'll never have a passionate love relationship with God if you allow His love letter to you to collect dust on a shelf.

Sure, there are many other books that can provide a few morsels of truth to guide you in your pursuit of sexual and emotional integrity, but books written by humans can only provide a certain amount of strength and spiritual nourishment. If you want to possess the power to guard your mind, body, heart, and soul, you need more than a few morsels of truth. You need a complete feast.

God's Word *is* that feast. His vast collection of truths can satisfy your craving for love and intimacy like nothing else can. His words hold the power to create universes, part seas, bring walls tumbling down, and totally transform even the most rebellious of hearts, including yours.

I promise
to love you forever

I find it ironic that in my pursuit of a man who could offer me the love I was longing for, I was overlooking the only One who could supply such love in abundance. Jesus patiently waited many years for me to recognize and respond to His passionate love.

Now that I've come to know Him not just as my Savior or my Friend but also as my heavenly Bridegroom, I've spent much time searching my soul to discover how I could have missed out on this intimacy for so long. Of course, my selfishness kept me blinded from His truth, but that was not all that had kept me from responding to Jesus' love for me.

When I peeled back multiple emotional layers, I realized that in my heart of hearts, I doubted that God could truly love me after all I had done. I knew that Jesus had to die for me to reconcile my sin, but I believed somehow that He had done it reluctantly, as something God required of Him. But as I've gotten to know Jesus, I've come to understand that He didn't save me because He had to. He saved me because He wanted to. He had a choice, and out of His passionate love for me, He chose to pay an incredibly high price so that we could spend eternity together. Now that is true love.

YOU HAVE MY UNCONDITIONAL LOVE

Do you need a personal revival and renewed sense of joy? Are you longing for a deeper level of intimacy and fulfillment than a husband

can possibly provide? Are you ready to bask in God's special love
for you and relish your role as His chosen bride? If so, carve out
some special time and a special place to run away and rendezvous
with your heavenly Bridegroom.

—*Every Woman's Battle*

Know therefore that the LORD your God is God; he is
the faithful God, keeping his covenant of love to a thou-
sand generations of those who love him and keep his
commands.

DEUTERONOMY 7:9

They refused to obey and didn't pay any attention to
the miracles you did for them; instead, they rebelled
and appointed a leader to take them back into slavery
in Egypt! But you are a God of forgiveness, always
ready to pardon, gracious and merciful, slow to become
angry, and full of love and mercy; you didn't abandon
them.

NEHEMIAH 9:17, TLB

Your love, O LORD, reaches to the heavens,
    your faithfulness to the skies.
Your righteousness is like the mighty mountains,
    your justice like the great deep....
    How priceless is your unfailing love!

Both high and low…
    find refuge in the shadow of your wings.
They feast on the abundance of your house;
    you give them drink from your river of
        delights.

PSALM 36:5-8

The LORD is gracious and merciful,
    slow to anger and abounding in steadfast love.
The LORD is good to all,
    and his compassion is over all that he has
        made.

PSALM 145:8-9, RSV

For long ago the Lord had said to Israel: "I have loved
you, O my people, with an everlasting love; with loving-
kindness I have drawn you to me."

JEREMIAH 31:3, TLB

I will plant her for myself in the land;
    I will show my love to the one I called "Not my
        loved one."
I will say to those called "Not my people,"
        "You are my people";
    and they will say, "You are my God."

HOSEA 2:23

Then I will cure you of idolatry and faithlessness, and my
love will know no bounds, for my anger will be forever
gone!

HOSEA 14:4, TLB

The LORD your God is with you,
    he is mighty to save.
He will take great delight in you,
    he will quiet you with his love,
    he will rejoice over you with singing.

ZEPHANIAH 3:17

My response is to get down on my knees before the
Father, this magnificent Father who parcels out all
heaven and earth. I ask him to strengthen you by
his Spirit—not a brute strength but a glorious inner
strength—that Christ will live in you as you open the
door and invite him in. And I ask him that with both
feet planted firmly on love, you'll be able to take in with
all Christians the extravagant dimensions of Christ's love.
Reach out and experience the breadth! Test its length!
Plumb the depths! Rise to the heights! Live full lives, full
in the fullness of God.

God can do anything, you know—far more than
you could ever imagine or guess or request in your
wildest dreams! He does it not by pushing us around

but by working within us, his Spirit deeply and gently
within us.

EPHESIANS 3:14-20, MSG

This is how God showed his love among us: He sent
his one and only Son into the world that we might
live through him. This is love: not that we loved
God, but that he loved us and sent his Son as an
atoning sacrifice for our sins. Dear friends, since
God so loved us, we also ought to love one another.
No one has ever seen God; but if we love one another,
God lives in us and his love is made complete in us.

We know that we live in him and he in us, because
he has given us of his Spirit. And we have seen and
testify that the Father has sent his Son to be the
Savior of the world. If anyone acknowledges that
Jesus is the Son of God, God lives in him and he
in God. And so we know and rely on the love God
has for us.

1 JOHN 4:9-16

I PROMISE TO BE A FOREVER FRIEND TO YOU

Love and mutual concern is the basis for a friend's relationship
with another friend. Jesus spoke very clearly to His disciples about

this deeper level of intimacy that He shared with them when He said, "I no longer call you servants, because a servant does not know his master's [personal] business. Instead, I have called you friends, for everything that I learned from my Father I have made known to you" (John 15:15). Jesus is saying, "I value you, not just because of how you serve me, but because you share my heart." A friend's value lies not so much in what she does, but in who she is as a personal confidant. God wants to be our friend, and He wants us as His friend.

—*Every Woman's Battle*

Even now my witness is in heaven;
　　　my advocate is on high.
My intercessor is my friend
　　　as my eyes pour out tears to God;
on behalf of a [woman] he pleads with God
　　　as a man pleads for his friend.

JOB 16:19-21

[She] who loves purity of heart
And has grace on [her] lips,
The king will be [her] friend.

PROVERBS 22:11, NKJV

As the Father has loved me, so have I loved you. Now remain in my love. If you obey my commands, you will

remain in my love, just as I have obeyed my Father's commands and remain in his love. I have told you this so that
my joy may be in you and that your joy may be complete.
My command is this: Love each other as I have loved you.
Greater love has no one than this, that he lay down his life
for his friends. You are my friends if you do what I command. I no longer call you servants, because a servant
does not know his master's business. Instead, I have called
you friends, for everything that I learned from my Father
I have made known to you.

JOHN 15:9-15

You see that faith was active along with his works, and
faith was completed by works, and the scripture was fulfilled which says, "Abraham believed God, and it was
reckoned to him as righteousness"; and he was called the
friend of God.

JAMES 2:22-23, RSV

I WILL ALWAYS BE YOUR HEAVENLY FATHER

As we realize and accept the truth that we are not just God's lump
of clay, sheep, servant, or even friend, but also God's very own
child, we can experience tremendous healing from childhood
wounds and disappointments. We can allow God to be the Father

or the Mother (He possesses qualities of both genders) that we so desperately need or want. We can be freed from the burden of trying to perform or produce for Him when we understand that He loves us not for what we do, but because of who we are as His daughters.

—*Every Woman's Battle*

And Jesus prayed this prayer: "O Father, Lord of heaven and earth, thank you for hiding the truth from those who think themselves so wise, and for revealing it to little children. Yes, Father, for it pleased you to do it this way!"

MATTHEW 11:25-26, TLB

Which of you fathers, if your son asks for a fish, will give him a snake instead? Or if he asks for an egg, will give him a scorpion? If you then, though you are evil, know how to give good gifts to your children, how much more will your Father in heaven give the Holy Spirit to those who ask him!

LUKE 11:11-13

Consider how the lilies grow. They do not labor or spin. Yet I tell you, not even Solomon in all his splendor was dressed like one of these. If that is how God clothes the grass of the field, which is here today, and tomorrow is thrown into the fire, how much more will he clothe you, O you of little faith! And do not set your heart on what you will eat or drink; do not worry about it. For the pagan world runs after all such things, and your Father knows that you need them. But seek his kingdom, and these things will be given to you as well.

Do not be afraid, little flock, for your Father has been pleased to give you the kingdom.

LUKE 12:27-32

If anyone serves Me, let [her] follow Me; and where I am, there My servant will be also. If anyone serves Me, [her] My Father will honor.

JOHN 12:26, NKJV

We tell you the good news: What God promised our fathers he has fulfilled for us, their children, by raising up Jesus. As it is written in the second Psalm: "You are my [child]; today I have become your Father."

ACTS 13:32-33

Yet for us there is but one God, the Father, from whom all things came and for whom we live; and there is but one Lord, Jesus Christ, through whom all things came and through whom we live.

1 CORINTHIANS 8:6

I will welcome you, and be a Father to you, and you will
be my sons and daughters.

2 CORINTHIANS 6:17-18, TLB

But when the time had fully come, God sent his Son, born
of a woman, born under law, to redeem those under law,
that we might receive the full rights of [daughters]. Because
you are [daughters], God sent the Spirit of his Son into
our hearts, the Spirit who calls out, "Abba, Father."

GALATIANS 4:4-6

Blessed be the God and Father of our Lord Jesus Christ,
who has blessed us in Christ with every spiritual blessing
in the heavenly places, even as he chose us in him before
the foundation of the world, that we should be holy and
blameless before him. He destined us in love to be his
[daughters] through Jesus Christ, according to the purpose of his will, to the praise of his glorious grace which
he freely bestowed on us in the Beloved.

EPHESIANS 1:3-6, RSV

For through him we both have access to the Father by
one Spirit. Consequently, you are no longer foreigners
and aliens, but fellow citizens with God's people and
members of God's household, built on the foundation of
the apostles and prophets, with Christ Jesus himself as the

chief cornerstone. In him the whole building is joined together and rises to become a holy temple in the Lord. And in him you too are being built together to become a dwelling in which God lives by his Spirit.

EPHESIANS 2:18-22

How great is the love the Father has lavished on us, that we should be called children of God! And that is what we are! The reason the world does not know us is that it did not know him. Dear friends, now we are children of God, and what we will be has not yet been made known. But we know that when he appears, we shall be like him, for we shall see him as he is.

1 JOHN 3:1-2

I PROMISE TO RETURN FOR YOU, MY BRIDE

Once a woman becomes a bride, the focus of her life and priorities change and all other people and priorities pale in comparison to this primary love relationship. Again, this metaphor illustrates a much deeper truth—God desires a level of relationship with us such that we are deeply in love with Him, that we delight to simply be in His presence, that we know Him personally both publicly and privately, and that our focus and priorities become aligned with His desires.

—*Every Woman's Battle*

You have stolen my heart, my sister, my bride;

 you have stolen my heart

with one glance of your eyes,

 with one jewel of your necklace.

How delightful is your love, my sister, my bride!

 How much more pleasing is your love than wine,

 and the fragrance of your perfume than any spice!

Your lips drop sweetness as the honeycomb, my bride;

 milk and honey are under your tongue.

SONG OF SOLOMON 4:9-11

I will greatly rejoice in the LORD,

 my soul shall exult in my God;

for he has clothed me with the garments of salvation,

 he has covered me with the robe of righteousness,

as a bridegroom decks himself with a garland,

 and as a bride adorns herself with her jewels.

ISAIAH 61:10, RSV

The nations shall see your righteousness. Kings shall be blinded by your glory; and God will confer on you a new name. He will hold you aloft in his hands for all to see— a splendid crown for the King of kings. Never again shall you be called "The God-forsaken Land" or the "Land that God Forgot." Your new name will be "The Land of God's Delight" and "The Bride," for the Lord delights in you and will claim you as his own. Your children will care for you, O Jerusalem, with joy like that of a young man who marries a virgin; and God will rejoice over you as a bridegroom with his bride.

ISAIAH 62:2-5, TLB

I will betroth you to me forever;
>   I will betroth you in righteousness and justice,
>   in love and compassion.
I will betroth you in faithfulness,
>   and you will acknowledge the LORD.

HOSEA 2:19-20

To this John replied, "A man can receive only what is given him from heaven. You yourselves can testify that I said, 'I am not the Christ but am sent ahead of him.' The bride belongs to the bridegroom. The friend who attends the bridegroom waits and listens for him, and is full of joy when he hears the bridegroom's voice. That joy is mine, and it is now complete. He must become greater; I must become less."

JOHN 3:27-30

Let us be glad and rejoice and give Him glory, for the marriage of the Lamb has come, and His wife has made herself ready. And to her it was granted to be arrayed in

fine linen, clean and bright, for the fine linen is the righteous acts of the saints.

Then he said to me, "Write: 'Blessed are those who
are called to the marriage supper of the Lamb!' " And he
said to me, "These are the true sayings of God."

REVELATION 19:7-9, NKJV

NOTHING WILL EVER SEPARATE YOU FROM MY LOVE

Don and Deyon Stephens, cofounders of Mercy Ships International, tell of Don's Aunt Lilly, who had a regular walking date with
God at 4 p.m. every day. "If you were visiting and Aunt Lilly disap-
peared around four o'clock, you just knew where she was going
and that she'd be back around five. She never allowed anything to
keep her from her date with Jesus." Aunt Lilly died within the past
few years, and when Don was preparing to preach her funeral, he
inquired as to the exact time of her death. His suspicion was con-
firmed when the hospital stated her time of death as 4 p.m. Aunt
Lilly didn't miss her walk with Jesus.

—*Every Woman's Battle*

Many are the woes of the wicked,
	but the LORD'S unfailing love
	surrounds the [woman] who trusts in him.

PSALM 32:10

But the eyes of the LORD are on those who fear him,
on those whose hope is in his unfailing love.

PSALM 33:18

I was so foolish and ignorant—
I must have seemed like a senseless animal to you.
Yet I still belong to you;
you are holding my right hand.

PSALM 73:22-23, NLT

The name of the LORD is a strong tower;
the righteous [woman] runs into it and is safe.

PROVERBS 18:10, RSV

"Though the mountains be shaken
and the hills be removed,
yet my unfailing love for you will not be shaken
nor my covenant of peace be removed,"
says the LORD, who has compassion on you.

ISAIAH 54:10

If God is for us, who can be against us?

ROMANS 8:31

Do you think anyone is going to be able to drive a wedge
between us and Christ's love for us? There is no way! Not

trouble, not hard times, not hatred, not hunger, not
homelessness, not bullying threats, not backstabbing, not
even the worst sins listed in Scripture.... None of this
fazes us because Jesus loves us. I'm absolutely convinced
that nothing—nothing living or dead, angelic or demonic,
today or tomorrow, high or low, thinkable or unthink-
able—absolutely nothing can get between us and God's
love because of the way that Jesus our Master has
embraced us.

ROMANS 8:35,37-39, MSG

I promise
to draw near to those
who draw near to Me

Up until a few years ago, I felt guilty and broken because of my sexual and emotional compromise. I thought I needed to get my life together before I could be in a genuine relationship with God. I tried and tried to walk the straight and narrow, but again and again I stumbled and fell back into compromising patterns.

Yet all that time God was holding out His gift of love to me and asking, "What are you waiting for?" He was eager for me to open and receive His gift of love, a love that could transform me, but I felt so unworthy that I left the gift unopened and in the basement for years. I thought I should earn such a gift before accepting it.

However, none of us can get our lives together on our own, apart from this love He offers. If you have felt unworthy of God's lavish love, you are right—you don't deserve it. No one does. But God's love for us is not based on our goodness. His love is based on His goodness.

I WILL NOT DISAPPOINT THOSE WHO PUT ME FIRST

While avoiding unhealthy emotional connections and relationships is important, it's not enough to guarantee success in keeping our hearts guarded against compromise. The secret to ultimate emotional satisfaction is to pursue a mad, passionate love relationship with the One who made our hearts, the One who purifies our hearts, and the One who strengthens our hearts against worldly temptations. The secret is to focus your heart on your First Love....

He wants your thoughts to turn to Him throughout the good

and the bad days. He wants you to watch for Him expectantly, so that you sense Him beckoning you into His presence. He aches for you to call out to Him and listen for His loving reply. Although He wants you to invest in healthy relationships with others, He wants you to be most concerned about your relationship with Him.

—*Every Woman's Battle*

I am GOD, your God, who brought you out of the land
    of Egypt, out of a life of slavery.
No other gods, only me.
No carved gods of any size, shape, or form of anything
    whatever, whether of things that fly or walk or swim.
    Don't bow down to them and don't serve them
    because I am GOD your God, and I'm a most jealous
    God, punishing the children for any sins their parents
    pass on to them to the third, and yes, even to the
    fourth generation of those who hate me. But I'm
    unswervingly loyal to the thousands who love me and
    keep my commandments.

EXODUS 20:2-6, MSG

Yes, the Almighty will be your gold
    And your precious silver;
For then you will have your delight in the Almighty,
    And lift up your face to God.

JOB 22:25-26, NKJV

Because [she] cleaves to me in love, I will deliver [her];

I will protect [her], because [she] knows my name.

When [she] calls to me, I will answer [her];

I will be with [her] in trouble,

I will rescue [her] and honor [her].

With long life I will satisfy [her],

and show [her] my salvation.

PSALM 91:14-16, RSV

For thou, O LORD, art most high over all the earth;

thou art exalted far above all gods.

The LORD loves those who hate evil;

he preserves the lives of his saints;

he delivers them from the hand of the wicked.

Light dawns for the righteous,

and joy for the upright in heart.

Rejoice in the LORD, O you righteous,

and give thanks to his holy name!

PSALM 97:9-12, RSV

I love those who love me,

and those who seek me find me.

With me are riches and honor,

enduring wealth and prosperity.

My fruit is better than fine gold;

what I yield surpasses choice silver.

I walk in the way of righteousness,
     along the paths of justice,
bestowing wealth on those who love me
     and making their treasuries full.

PROVERBS 8:17-21

The God who made the world and everything in it, this
Master of sky and land, doesn't live in custom-made
shrines or need the human race to run errands for him, as
if he couldn't take care of himself. He makes the creatures;
the creatures don't make him. Starting from scratch, he
made the entire human race and made the earth hos-
pitable, with plenty of time and space for living so we
could seek after God, and not just grope around in the
dark but actually find him. He doesn't play hide-and-seek
with us. He's not remote; he's near. We live and move in
him, can't get away from him!

ACTS 17:24-28, MSG

Whoever has my commands and obeys them, [she] is the
one who loves me. [She] who loves me will be loved by my
Father, and I too will love [her] and show myself to [her].

JOHN 14:21

May God give peace to you, my Christian [sisters], and
love, with faith from God the Father and the Lord Jesus

Christ. May God's grace and blessing be upon all who sincerely love our Lord Jesus Christ.

EPHESIANS 6:23-24, TLB

I PROMISE TO LISTEN WHEN YOU PRAY

As I confess, I often sense Him comforting me, saying, "It's okay. I'm not going to let that come between us." As I ask Him for guidance, He usually steers my mind toward a solution I hadn't thought of before. As I pray for others, He regularly prompts me to do or say something specifically for their benefit. This response time is a vital part of my prayer life. He already knows what is on my heart without my saying a word.... Sometimes...I'll sense God saying, "Remember to leave Me some time. I've got a lot I want to say to you today." Does this make me feel special that the God of the universe wants time to talk specifically with me each day? You bet. And He wants to talk with you each day as well.

—*Every Woman's Battle*

The LORD hears the needy
and does not despise his captive people.

PSALM 69:33

For the eyes of the Lord are intently watching all who live good lives, and he gives attention when they cry to him.

But the Lord has made up his mind to wipe out even the
memory of evil men [and women] from the earth. Yes, the
Lord hears the good [woman] when [she] calls to him for
help and saves [her] out of all [her] troubles.

PSALM 34:15-17, TLB

The LORD is righteous in all his ways
    and loving toward all he has made.
The LORD is near to all who call on him,
    to all who call on him in truth.
He fulfills the desires of those who fear him;
    he hears their cry and saves them.
The LORD watches over all who love him,
    but all the wicked he will destroy.
My mouth will speak in praise of the LORD.
    Let every creature praise his holy name
    for ever and ever.

PSALM 145:17-21

The LORD is far from the wicked
    but he hears the prayer of the righteous.

PROVERBS 15:29

O my people in Jerusalem, you shall weep no more, for
he will surely be gracious to you at the sound of your cry.

He will answer you. Though he give you the bread of adversity and water of affliction, yet he will be with you to teach you—with your own eyes you will see your Teacher. And if you leave God's paths and go astray, you will hear a Voice behind you say, "No, this is the way; walk here."

ISAIAH 30:19-21, TLB

If you do these things, God will shed his own glorious light upon you. He will heal you; your godliness will lead you forward, goodness will be a shield before you, and the glory of the Lord will protect you from behind. Then, when you call, the Lord will answer. "Yes, I am here," he will quickly reply.

ISAIAH 58:8-9, TLB

It shall come to pass
That before they call, I will answer;
And while they are still speaking, I will hear.

ISAIAH 65:24, NKJV

"Then you will call upon me and come and pray to me, and I will listen to you. You will seek me and find me when you seek me with all your heart. I will be found by you," declares the LORD, "and will bring you back from captivity. I will gather you from all the nations and places where I have banished you," declares the LORD, "and will bring you back to the place from which I carried you into exile."

JEREMIAH 29:12-14

Call to Me, and I will answer you, and show you great and mighty things, which you do not know.

JEREMIAH 33:3, NKJV

I will bring the third that remain through the fire and make them pure, as gold and silver are refined and purified by fire. They will call upon my name and I will hear them; I will say, "These are my people," and they will say, "The Lord is our God."

ZECHARIAH 13:9, TLB

But when you pray, do not be like the hypocrites, for they love to pray standing in the synagogues and on the street corners to be seen by men. I tell you the truth, they have received their reward in full. But when you pray, go into your room, close the door and pray to your Father, who is unseen. Then your Father, who sees what is done in secret, will reward you.

MATTHEW 6:5-6

Your Father knows what you need before you ask him.

This, then, is how you should pray:

"Our Father in heaven,
hallowed be your name,
your kingdom come,
your will be done
> on earth as it is in heaven.
Give us today our daily bread.
Forgive us our debts,
> as we also have forgiven our debtors.
And lead us not into temptation,
but deliver us from the evil one."

MATTHEW 6:8-13

Ask, and it will be given to you; seek, and you will find; knock, and it will be opened to you. For everyone who asks receives, and he who seeks finds, and to him who knocks it will be opened. Or what man is there among you who, if his son asks for bread, will give him a stone? Or if he asks for a fish, will he give him a serpent? If you then, being evil, know how to give good gifts to your children, how much more will your Father who is in heaven give good things to those who ask Him!

MATTHEW 7:7-11, NKJV

Then Jesus told them, "I assure you, if you have faith and don't doubt, you can do things like this and much more. You can even say to this mountain, 'May God lift you up and throw you into the sea,' and it will happen. If you believe, you will receive whatever you ask for in prayer."

MATTHEW 21:21-22, NLT

Truly, truly, I say to you, he who believes in me will also do the works that I do; and greater works than these will he do, because I go to the Father. Whatever you ask in my name, I will do it, that the Father may be glorified in the Son; if you ask anything in my name, I will do it.

JOHN 14:12-14, RSV

In that day you will no longer ask me anything. I tell you the truth, my Father will give you whatever you ask in my name. Until now you have not asked for anything in my name. Ask and you will receive, and your joy will be complete.

JOHN 16:23-24

In the same way, the Spirit helps us in our weakness. We do not know what we ought to pray for, but the Spirit himself intercedes for us with groans that words cannot express. And he who searches our hearts knows the mind

of the Spirit, because the Spirit intercedes for the saints in
accordance with God's will.

ROMANS 8:26-27

In him and through faith in him we may approach God
with freedom and confidence.

EPHESIANS 3:12

I have written this to you who believe in the Son of God
so that you may know you have eternal life. And we are
sure of this, that he will listen to us whenever we ask
him for anything in line with his will. And if we really
know he is listening when we talk to him and make our
requests, then we can be sure that he will answer us.

1 JOHN 5:13-15, TLB

I WILL SHOW YOU I AM TRUSTWORTHY

It seemed that my faith was being put to the test. Could I trust that
this direction was truly from God, or was my mind playing tricks on
me? Could I practice what I was preaching about remaining sexually pure, or would I indulge in living a double life? Could I leave
John without looking back, or had he become an idol that I would
cling to? Did I want to resist extramarital temptation enough to give
up my ministry, sell my dream house, leave my extended family and

friends, and move to a place where nothing was familiar to me? Or did I want to hold on to my own kingdom and stay in my comfort zone? These and tons of other questions whirled around in my mind, but they all boiled down to these: Who did I love more? Who did I trust more? Who would I follow? God or John?

—*Every Woman's Battle*

Praise be to the LORD, who has given rest to his people Israel just as he promised. Not one word has failed of all the good promises he gave through his servant Moses. May the LORD our God be with us as he was with our fathers; may he never leave us nor forsake us.... But your hearts must be fully committed to the LORD our God, to live by his decrees and obey his commands, as at this time.

1 KINGS 8:56-57,61

Trust in the LORD and do good.
    Then you will live safely in the land and prosper.
Take delight in the LORD,
    and he will give you your heart's desires.
Commit everything you do to the LORD.
    Trust him, and he will help you.
He will make your innocence as clear as the dawn,
    and the justice of your cause will shine like the
        noonday sun.

PSALM 37:3-6, NLT

He has given me a new song to sing, of praises to our God. Now many will hear of the glorious things he did for me, and stand in awe before the Lord, and put their trust in him. Many blessings are given to those who trust the Lord and have no confidence in those who are proud or who trust in idols.

O Lord my God, many and many a time you have done great miracles for us, and we are ever in your thoughts. Who else can do such glorious things? No one else can be compared with you. There isn't time to tell of all your wonderful deeds.

PSALM 40:3-5, TLB

I don't need the bulls you sacrifice;
    I don't need the blood of goats.
What I want instead is your true thanks to God;
    I want you to fulfill your vows to the Most High.
Trust me in your times of trouble,
    and I will rescue you,
    and you will give me glory.

PSALM 50:13-15, NLT

Cast your cares on the LORD
    and he will sustain you;
    he will never let the righteous fall.

PSALM 55:22

Praise the Lord! For all who fear God and trust in him are blessed beyond expression. Yes, happy is the [woman] who delights in doing his commands. [Her] children shall be honored everywhere, for good [women's] sons [and daughters] have a special heritage. [She herself] shall be wealthy, and [her] good deeds will never be forgotten.

PSALM 112:1-3, TLB

Such people will not be overcome by evil circumstances.

Those who are righteous will be long remembered.

They do not fear bad news;

they confidently trust the LORD to care for them.

They are confident and fearless

and can face their foes triumphantly.

They give generously to those in need.

Their good deeds will never be forgotten.

They will have influence and honor.

PSALM 112:6-9, NLT

Those who trust in the Lord

Are like Mount Zion,

Which cannot be moved, but abides forever.

As the mountains surround Jerusalem,

So the LORD surrounds His people

From this time forth and forever.

PSALM 125:1-2, NKJV

Never forget the things I've taught you. If you want a long and satisfying life, closely follow my instructions. Never tire of loyalty and kindness. Hold these virtues tightly. Write them deep within your heart. If you want favor with both God and man, and a reputation for good judgment and common sense, then trust the Lord completely; don't ever trust yourself. In everything you do, put God first, and he will direct you and crown your efforts with success.

PROVERBS 3:1-6, TLB

The LORD is good,
    a refuge in times of trouble.
He cares for those who trust in him.

NAHUM 1:7

I know how to be abased, and I know how to abound. Everywhere and in all things I have learned both to be full and to be hungry, both to abound and to suffer need. I can do all things through Christ who strengthens me.

PHILIPPIANS 4:12-13, NKJV

Now we can look forward to the salvation God has promised us. There is no longer any room for doubt, and we can tell others that salvation is ours, for there is no question that he will do what he says.

HEBREWS 10:23, TLB

I WILL NEVER ABANDON YOU

The same God whose words possessed the power to form the entire universe longs to whisper into your hungry heart words that have the power to thrill you, heal you, and draw you into a deeper love relationship than you ever imagined possible. A guy may say that you look fine, but God's Word says, "The king is enthralled by your beauty" (Psalm 45:11). A man may tell you, "Of course I love you," but God says, "I have loved you with an everlasting love; I have drawn you with loving-kindness" (Jeremiah 31:3). Even your husband may tell you, "I'm committed to you until death," but God says, "Never will I leave you; never will I forsake you" (Hebrews 13:5).

—*Every Woman's Battle*

When you are in distress, and all these things come upon
you in the latter days, when you turn to the LORD your God
and obey His voice (for the LORD your God is a merciful
God), He will not forsake you nor destroy you, nor forget
the covenant of your fathers which He swore to them.

DEUTERONOMY 4:30-31, NKJV

I once was young, now I'm a graybeard—
    not once have I seen an abandoned believer,
    or his kids out roaming the streets.
Every day he's out giving and lending,
    his children making him proud.

Turn your back on evil,

work for the good and don't quit.

GOD loves this kind of thing,

never turns away from his friends.

PSALM 37:25-28, MSG

I know what I'm doing. I have it all planned out—plans to take care of you, not abandon you, plans to give you the future you hope for.

JEREMIAH 29:11, MSG

I will ask the Father, and he will give you another Counselor to be with you forever—the Spirit of truth. The world cannot accept him, because it neither sees him nor knows him. But you know him, for he lives with you and will be in you. I will not leave you as orphans; I will come to you. Before long, the world will not see me anymore, but you will see me. Because I live, you also will live. On that day you will realize that I am in my Father, and you are in me, and I am in you.

JOHN 14:16-20

Be content with what you have, because God has said, "Never will I leave you;

never will I forsake you."

HEBREWS 13:5

I promise to help you resist the enemy

Satan's schemes can really throw us for a loop. He often knows our weaknesses, and his temptations can come in such seductive packages. We're sometimes blindsided by sin and only recognize Satan's activity in our lives in hindsight, usually when we are left reeling from its destructive consequences.

I believe people make one of two errors when it comes to judging Satan's power to lure us into temptation. We either underestimate him, dismissing the authority he and his demons have in this present world, or we overestimate him and live in constant fear of falling into his traps. We also make the mistake of giving Satan too much credit, blaming our own fleshly desires on his activity.

But with a balanced view of Satan, we can recognize his limited power and exercise our own authority over him as believers in Christ. Remember, he's a supernatural being, but he's not God. He's not omnipresent or omniscient, so he can't be everywhere at all times or know what you are thinking the way God can. Rather than focus on Satan's schemes and live in fear, let us focus on our faithful protector, Jesus Christ.

I'VE ALREADY DEFEATED THE ENEMY FOR YOU

The devil knew he now possessed this gift [of authority], and so did God. Satan actually flaunted his authority in front of Jesus' face, daring Him to try to take it back by playing Satan's twisted game rather than submitting to God's plan of restoring the gift of authority to humankind (a plan that would require the shedding of His blood unto death)....

Notice [in Luke 4:5-8] that Jesus didn't deny the devil's *current* authority over the kingdoms of the earth. But He knew what the future held, and that it was just a matter of time before that authority would change hands and be returned to the rightful owner. He knew that He could never sin and win that authority back, therefore Jesus chose God's plan to restore and entrust that authority to humanity once again through His death and resurrection and the coming of the Holy Spirit.

—*Every Woman's Battle*

Do not let your heart faint, do not be afraid, and do not tremble or be terrified because of them; for the LORD your God is He who goes with you, to fight for you against your enemies, to save you.

DEUTERONOMY 20:3-4, NKJV

But now thus says the LORD,
    he who created you, O Jacob,
    he who formed you, O Israel:
"Fear not, for I have redeemed you;
    I have called you by name, you are mine.
When you pass through the waters I will be with you;
    and through the rivers, they shall not overwhelm you;

when you walk through fire you shall not be burned,
    and the flame shall not consume you."

ISAIAH 43:1-2, RSV

I have told you these things, so that in me you may have
peace. In this world you will have trouble. But take heart!
I have overcome the world.

JOHN 16:33

Praise be to the Lord, the God of Israel,
    because he has come and has redeemed
        his people.
He has raised up a horn of salvation for us
    in the house of his servant David
(as he said through his holy prophets of long
        ago),
salvation from our enemies
    and from the hand of all who hate us—
to show mercy to our fathers
    and to remember his holy covenant,
    the oath he swore to our father Abraham:
to rescue us from the hand of our enemies,
    and to enable us to serve him without fear
    in holiness and righteousness before him all
        our days.

LUKE 1:68-75

[Jesus] said to them, "I saw Satan fall like lightning from heaven. Behold, I give you the authority to trample on serpents and scorpions, and over all the power of the enemy, and nothing shall by any means hurt you."

LUKE 10:18-19, NKJV

Submit yourselves, then, to God. Resist the devil, and he will flee from you. Come near to God and he will come near to you.

JAMES 4:7-8

I WILL BE YOUR BODYGUARD

You are getting into a four-door car by yourself. It's late at night and you are in a rough neighborhood. In order to feel safe, what is the first thing you are going to do when you get in the car? Right. Lock the doors.

How many doors will you lock? You may think this is a silly question, but think about it. If you only locked one or two or even three of the doors, would you be safe? Of course not. All four doors must be locked to keep out an unwelcome intruder.

The same is true with keeping out unwelcome sexual temptations.... Even if we leave only one [door] unlocked, we are vulnerable. We must guard all four areas (our minds, our hearts, our mouths, and our bodies) to have any hope of remaining safe and maintaining sexual integrity.

—*Every Woman's Battle*

Many are asking, "Who can show us any good?"
>Let the light of your face shine upon us, O LORD.

You have filled my heart with greater joy
>than when their grain and new wine abound.

I will lie down and sleep in peace,
>for you alone, O LORD,
>make me dwell in safety.

>PSALM 4:6-8

The LORD is a stronghold for the oppressed,
>a stronghold in times of trouble.

And those who know thy name put their trust in thee,
>for thou, O LORD, hast not forsaken those who
>>seek thee.

Sing praises to the LORD, who dwells in Zion!
>Tell among the peoples his deeds!

For he who avenges blood is mindful of them;
>he does not forget the cry of the afflicted.

Be gracious to me, O LORD!
>Behold what I suffer from those who hate me,
>O thou who liftest me up from the gates of death,

that I may recount all thy praises,

that in the gates of the daughter of Zion

I may rejoice in thy deliverance.

PSALM 9:9-14, RSV

I love you, LORD; you are my strength.

The LORD is my rock, my fortress, and my savior;

my God is my rock, in whom I find protection.

He is my shield, the strength of my salvation,

and my stronghold.

I will call on the LORD, who is worthy of praise,

for he saves me from my enemies.

The ropes of death surrounded me;

the floods of destruction swept over me.

The grave wrapped its ropes around me;

death itself stared me in the face.

But in my distress I cried out to the LORD;

yes, I prayed to my God for help.

He heard me from his sanctuary;

my cry reached his ears.

PSALM 18:1-6, NLT

Shall I look to the mountain gods for help? No! My help is from Jehovah who made the mountains! And the heavens too! He will never let me stumble, slip, or fall. For he is always watching, never sleeping. Jehovah himself is car-

ing for you! He is your defender. He protects you day and
night. He keeps you from all evil and preserves your life.
He keeps his eye upon you as you come and go and
always guards you.

PSALM 121:1-8, TLB

My [daughter], preserve sound judgment and discernment,
    do not let them out of your sight;
they will be life for you,
    an ornament to grace your neck.
Then you will go on your way in safety,
    and your foot will not stumble;
when you lie down, you will not be afraid;
    when you lie down, your sleep will be sweet.
Have no fear of sudden disaster
    or of the ruin that overtakes the wicked,
for the LORD will be your confidence
    and will keep your foot from being snared.

PROVERBS 3:21-26

"But I will deliver you in that day," says the LORD, "and
you shall not be given into the hand of the men of whom
you are afraid. For I will surely deliver you, and you shall
not fall by the sword; but your life shall be as a prize to you,
because you have put your trust in Me," says the LORD.

JEREMIAH 39:17-18, NKJV

I WILL TAKE HOLD OF YOUR HAND
WHENEVER YOU COME TO ME FOR HELP

Getting to know God more intimately means, in part, learning how He feels about you and understanding the provisions He has made in order to satisfy your innermost desires to feel loved, needed, and powerful (a righteous form of power, not a manipulative one). This is a great way to discover who you really are—not as the world tries to program you to be, but as your Maker designed you to be. Once you allow God to correct your beliefs about yourself, those beliefs will begin driving your decisions, your behaviors will follow directly behind, and you will have victory in this battle against sexual compromise.

—*Every Woman's Battle*

Tell me what to do, O Lord, and make it plain because I am surrounded by waiting enemies. Don't let them get me, Lord! Don't let me fall into their hands! For they accuse me of things I never did, and all the while are plotting cruelty. I am expecting the Lord to rescue me again, so that once again I will see his goodness to me here in the land of the living. Don't be impatient. Wait for the Lord, and he will come and save you! Be brave, stouthearted, and courageous. Yes, wait and he will help you.

PSALM 27:11-14, TLB

O God, we meditate on your unfailing love
    as we worship in your Temple.
As your name deserves, O God,
    you will be praised to the ends of the earth.
    Your strong right hand is filled with victory.
Let the people on Mount Zion rejoice.
    Let the towns of Judah be glad,
    for your judgments are just.
Go, inspect the city of Jerusalem.
    Walk around and count the many towers.
Take note of the fortified walls,
    and tour all the citadels,
that you may describe them
    to future generations.
For that is what God is like.
    He is our God forever and ever,
    and he will be our guide until we die.

PSALM 48:9-14, NLT

Though the LORD is on high, he looks upon the lowly,
    but the proud he knows from afar.
Though I walk in the midst of trouble,
    you preserve my life;
you stretch out your hand against the anger of my foes,
    with your right hand you save me.

The LORD will fulfill [his purpose] for me;

    your love, O LORD, endures forever—

    do not abandon the works of your hands.

PSALM 138:6-8

I am holding you by your right hand—I, the Lord your God—and I say to you, Don't be afraid; I am here to help you. Despised though you are, fear not, O Israel; for I will help you. I am the Lord, your Redeemer; I am the Holy One of Israel.

ISAIAH 41:13-14, TLB

And I will lead the blind

    in a way that they know not,

in paths that they have not known

    I will guide them.

I will turn the darkness before them into light,

    the rough places into level ground.

These are the things I will do,

    and I will not forsake them.

ISAIAH 42:16, RSV

Let him have all your worries and cares, for he is always thinking about you and watching everything that concerns you.

1 PETER 5:7, TLB

But at the same time the Lord rescued Lot out of Sodom because he was a good man, sick of the terrible wickedness he saw everywhere around him day after day. So also the Lord can rescue you and me from the temptations that surround us.

2 PETER 2:7-9, TLB

I WILL HELP YOU CONTROL YOUR FLESHLY DESIRES

If you want to know how to satisfy your hunger for power (which is a normal part of the human condition but can certainly drive you much further into this battle than you want to go), I'll let you in on a secret: The sense of power that will satisfy your soul is not found in *men*. It is found only in *God*. Does God give His power to men? Yes. But do you need to go through a man to receive God's power? No. The only middleman you need to tap into God's power is the Holy Spirit. And when you discover the power of the Holy Spirit to help you live an abundantly fulfilled life, you will know that seductive power pales in comparison.

—*Every Woman's Battle*

Behold, happy is the [woman] whom God
    corrects;
Therefore do not despise the chastening of the
    Almighty.

For He bruises, but He binds up;
He wounds, but His hands make whole.

JOB 5:17-18, NKJV

But if you will look to God
and plead with the Almighty,
if you are pure and upright,
even now he will rouse himself on your behalf
and restore you to your rightful place.

JOB 8:5-6

Come to me, all you who are weary and burdened, and I will give you rest. Take my yoke upon you and learn from me, for I am gentle and humble in heart, and you will find rest for your souls. For my yoke is easy and my burden is light.

MATTHEW 11:28-30

Therefore do not let sin reign in your mortal body so that you obey its evil desires. Do not offer the parts of your body to sin, as instruments of wickedness, but rather offer yourselves to God, as those who have been brought from death to life; and offer the parts of your body to him as instruments of righteousness. For sin shall not be your master, because you are not under law, but under grace.

ROMANS 6:12-14

So there is now no condemnation awaiting those who belong to Christ Jesus. For the power of the life-giving Spirit—and this power is mine through Christ Jesus—has freed me from the vicious circle of sin and death. We aren't saved from sin's grasp by knowing the commandments of God, because we can't and don't keep them, but God put into effect a different plan to save us. He sent his own Son in a human body like ours—except that ours are sinful—and destroyed sin's control over us by giving himself as a sacrifice for our sins. So now we can obey God's laws if we follow after the Holy Spirit and no longer obey the old evil nature within us.

ROMANS 8:1-4, TLB

As for you, you were dead in your transgressions and sins, in which you used to live when you followed the ways of this world and of the ruler of the kingdom of the air, the spirit who is now at work in those who are disobedient. All of us also lived among them at one time, gratifying the cravings of our sinful nature and following its desires and thoughts. Like the rest, we were by nature objects of wrath. But because of his great love for us, God, who is rich in mercy, made us alive with Christ even when we were dead in transgressions—it is by grace you have been saved.

EPHESIANS 2:1-5

When you came to Christ, you were "circumcised,"
but not by a physical procedure. It was a spiritual
procedure—the cutting away of your sinful nature. For
you were buried with Christ when you were baptized.
And with him you were raised to a new life because you
trusted the mighty power of God, who raised Christ
from the dead.

COLOSSIANS 2:11-12, NLT

So don't feel sorry for yourselves. Or have you forgotten
how good parents treat children, and that God regards
you as his children?

My dear child, don't shrug off God's discipline,
    but don't be crushed by it either.
It's the child he loves that he disciplines;
    the child he embraces, he also corrects.

God is educating you; that's why you must never drop
out. He's treating you as dear children. This trouble
you're in isn't punishment; it's training, the normal
experience of children. Only irresponsible parents leave
children to fend for themselves. Would you prefer an
irresponsible God? We respect our own parents for training and not spoiling us, so why not embrace God's training so we can truly live? While we were children, our

parents did what seemed best to them. But God is doing what is best for us, training us to live God's holy best.

HEBREWS 12:5-10, MSG

As we know Jesus better, his divine power gives us everything we need for living a godly life. He has called us to receive his own glory and goodness! And by that same mighty power, he has given us all of his rich and wonderful promises. He has promised that you will escape the decadence all around you caused by evil desires and that you will share in his divine nature.

2 PETER 1:3-4, NLT

Do not love the world or the things in the world. If any one loves the world, love for the Father is not in him. For all that is in the world, the lust of the flesh and the lust of the eyes and the pride of life, is not of the Father but is of the world. And the world passes away, and the lust of it; but he who does the will of God abides for ever.

1 JOHN 2:15-17, RSV

I PROMISE TO HELP YOU FIND A WAY OUT WHEN YOU ARE TEMPTED

Paul tells us in 1 Corinthians 10:13, "No temptation has seized you except what is common to [woman]. And God is faithful; he will not let you be tempted beyond what you can bear. But when you are tempted, he will also provide a way out so that you can stand up under it." Paul didn't say, "If you experience sexual temptation, there must be something wrong with you because no one else struggles with it that much." He said that all temptations are common. And because God creates all human beings (regardless of gender, nationality, or economic background) as sexual human beings, you can bet that sexual and relational temptations are by far the most common temptations on the planet.

—*Every Woman's Battle*

For he has not despised or abhorred
    the affliction of the afflicted;
and he has not hid his face from [her]
    but has heard, when [she] cried to him.

PSALM 22:24, RSV

If the LORD delights in a [woman's] way,
    he makes [her] steps firm;
though [she] stumble, [she] will not fall,
    for the LORD upholds [her] with his hand.

PSALM 37:23-24

Then you called out to GOD in your desperate condition;
    he got you out in the nick of time.

He led you out of your dark, dark cell,
> broke open the jail and led you out.
So thank GOD for his marvelous love,
> for his miracle mercy to the children he loves;
He shattered the heavy jailhouse doors,
> he snapped the prison bars like matchsticks!

PSALM 107:13-16, MSG

I, the LORD, have called you in righteousness;
> I will take hold of your hand.
I will keep you and will make you
> to be a covenant for the people
> and a light for the Gentiles,
to open eyes that are blind,
> to free captives from prison
> and to release from the dungeon those who sit
> > in darkness.

ISAIAH 42:6-7

I WILL GIVE YOU POWER TO OVERCOME THE ENEMY

We do not accidentally *fall* in love or into sexual immorality. We either *dive* in that direction (either passively or aggressively), or we intentionally choose to turn the other way, refusing to cross the line between that which is fruitful and that which is forbidden. Although our emotions are very powerful, we do not have to allow them to drive our thoughts and actions into compromising situations. Instead, we can fall back on God's power to guard our hearts, driving our emotions into appropriate situations and relationships.

—*Every Woman's Battle*

The LORD is my light and my salvation;
    whom shall I fear?
The LORD is the stronghold of my life;
    of whom shall I be afraid?...
One thing have I asked of the LORD,
    that will I seek after;
that I may dwell in the house of the LORD,
    all the days of my life,
to behold the beauty of the LORD,
    and to inquire in his temple.
For he will hide me in his shelter
    in the day of trouble;
he will conceal me under the cover of his tent,
    he will set me high upon a rock.
And now my head shall be lifted up
    above my enemies round about me;
and I will offer in his tent
    sacrifices with shouts of joy;
I will sing and make melody to the LORD.

PSALM 27:1,4-6, RSV

How great is your goodness,

which you have stored up for those who fear you,

which you bestow in the sight of men

on those who take refuge in you.

In the shelter of your presence you hide them

from the intrigues of men;

in your dwelling you keep them safe

from accusing tongues.

Praise be to the LORD,

for he showed his wonderful love to me

when I was in a besieged city.

In my alarm I said,

"I am cut off from your sight!"

Yet you heard my cry for mercy

when I called to you for help.

Love the LORD, all his saints!

The LORD preserves the faithful.

PSALM 31:19-23

Have you not known? Have you not heard?

The LORD is the everlasting God,

the Creator of the ends of the earth.

He does not faint or grow weary,

his understanding is unsearchable.

He gives power to the faint,

and to him who has no might he increases strength.

Even youths shall faint and be weary,
    and young men shall fall exhausted;
but they who wait for the LORD shall renew their strength,
    they shall mount up with wings like eagles,
they shall run and not be weary,
    they shall walk and not faint.

ISAIAH 40:28-31, RSV

But in that coming day, no weapon turned against you shall succeed, and you will have justice against every courtroom lie. This is the heritage of the servants of the Lord. This is the blessing I have given you, says the Lord.

ISAIAH 54:17, TLB

If we get included in Christ's sin-conquering death, we also get included in his life-saving resurrection. We know that when Jesus was raised from the dead it was a signal of the end of death-as-the-end. Never again will death have the last word. When Jesus died, he took sin down with him, but alive he brings God down to us. From now on, think of it this way: Sin speaks a dead language that means nothing to you; God speaks your mother tongue, and you hang on every word. You are dead to sin and alive to God. That's what Jesus did.

ROMANS 6:8-11, MSG

If you forgive anyone, I also forgive him. And what I have forgiven—if there was anything to forgive—I have forgiven in the sight of Christ for your sake, in order that Satan might not outwit us. For we are not unaware of his schemes.

2 CORINTHIANS 2:10-11

I have been crucified with Christ: and I myself no longer live, but Christ lives in me. And the real life I now have within this body is a result of my trusting in the Son of God, who loved me and gave himself for me.

GALATIANS 2:20, TLB

For our struggle is not against flesh and blood, but against the rulers, against the authorities, against the powers of this dark world and against the spiritual forces of evil in the heavenly realms. Therefore put on the full armor of God, so that when the day of evil comes, you may be able to stand your ground, and after you have done everything, to stand. Stand firm then, with the belt of truth buckled around your waist, with the breastplate of righteousness in place, and with your feet fitted with the readiness that comes from the gospel of peace. In addition to all this, take up the shield of faith, with which you can extinguish all the flaming arrows of the evil one. Take the helmet of salvation and the sword of the Spirit, which is the word of God.

EPHESIANS 6:12-17

In a great house there are not only vessels of gold and silver but also of wood and earthenware, and some for noble use, some for ignoble. If any one purifies [herself] from what is ignoble, then [she] will be a vessel for noble use, consecrated and useful to the master of the house, ready for any good work. So shun youthful passions and aim at righteousness, faith, love, and peace, along with those who call upon the Lord from a pure heart.

2 Timothy 2:20-22, rsv

I promise you
sweet surrender

For me, the hardest part of any trip is the unpacking. It seems I always return with far more stuff than I left the house with. Sometimes it takes days before I find a proper place for everything to land, but then I get the satisfaction of putting that empty suitcase away and declaring my unpacking done!

There's another kind of suitcase that many of us also struggle with unpacking on a daily basis, and that's our emotional baggage. It seems we can't always find an appropriate place for all of our insecurities, wounds, and fears, so we leave them inside where they become a heavy load for us to drag around through life.

At the end of each day, my husband and I often pray about all the things in our lives that we really don't know what to do with. We verbalize to God and to each other that we are placing them on the "God shelf," because we don't want to continue lugging them around.

As you read God's promises about surrender, I recommend that you mentally create your own God shelf. Imagine that it is big and sturdy enough for anything you could possibly pile on it, and rest assured that there's always room for your troubles on God's shelf!

I WILL HELP YOU LET GO OF PAST PAIN

If you want to win the battle for sexual integrity, you must let go of past emotional pain. Maybe a father who was absent, either emotionally or physically, wounded you. Maybe the distance in your relationship with your mother left you feeling desperately lonely. Perhaps your siblings or friends never treated you with dignity or respect. If you were abused in any way (physically, sexually, or verbally) as a child, maybe you have anger and pain that has yet to be reconciled.

Perhaps old lovers took advantage of your vulnerabilities, strung you along, or were unfaithful to you. Or maybe you've never understood why God allowed _____ to happen (you fill in the blank). Regardless of its source, we must surrender the pain from our past in order to stand strong in the battle for sexual and emotional integrity.

—*Every Woman's Battle*

He heals the brokenhearted
    and binds up their wounds.

PSALM 147:3

Lord, you alone can heal me, you alone can save, and my praises are for you alone.

JEREMIAH 17:14, TLB

"But all who devour you will be devoured;
    all your enemies will go into exile.
Those who plunder you will be plundered;
    all who make spoil of you I will despoil.

But I will restore you to health
and heal your wounds,"
    declares the LORD.

JEREMIAH 30:16-17

And Jesus went about all Galilee, teaching in their synagogues, preaching the gospel of the kingdom, and healing all
kinds of sickness and all kinds of disease among the people.

MATTHEW 4:23, NKJV

Is any one among you suffering? Let [her] pray. Is any cheer-
ful? Let [her] sing praise. Is any among you sick? Let [her]
call for the elders of the church, and let them pray over
[her], anointing [her] with oil in the name of the Lord; and
the prayer of faith will save the sick [woman], and the Lord
will raise [her] up; and if [she] has committed sins, [she] will
be forgiven. Therefore confess your sins to one another, and
pray for one another, that you may be healed. The prayer of
a righteous [woman] has great power in its effects.

JAMES 5:13-16, RSV

He never sinned, and he never deceived anyone. He did
not retaliate when he was insulted. When he suffered, he
did not threaten to get even. He left his case in the hands
of God, who always judges fairly. He personally carried

away our sins in his own body on the cross so we can
be dead to sin and live for what is right. You have been
healed by his wounds! Once you were wandering like lost
sheep. But now you have turned to your Shepherd, the
Guardian of your souls.

1 PETER 2:22-25, NLT

I WILL HELP YOU SURRENDER YOUR PRESENT PRIDE

I recently heard a statement that made my heart skip a beat: "You
are never more like Satan than when you are full of pride." Isn't it
true? Pride got Satan expelled from heaven. Pride hinders sinners
from asking Jesus to be their Savior and submitting to His lord-
ship. And pride keeps Christians from repenting from the things
that cause them to stumble and fall, such as sexual and emotional
compromise.

—*Every Woman's Battle*

Good and upright is the LORD;
      therefore he instructs sinners in the way.
He leads the humble in what is right,
      and teaches the humble his way.
All the paths of the LORD are steadfast love and faithfulness,
      for those who keep his covenant and his testimonies.

PSALM 25:8-10, RSV

[She] whose ear heeds wholesome admonition
>   will abide among the wise.
[She] who ignores instruction despises [herself],
>   but [she] who heeds admonition gains understanding.
The fear of the LORD is instruction in wisdom,
>   and humility goes before honor.

PROVERBS 15:31-33, RSV

To get wisdom is better than gold;
>   to get understanding is to be chosen rather than silver.
The highway of the upright turns aside from evil;
>   [she] who guards [her] way preserves [her] life.
Pride goes before destruction,
>   and a haughty spirit before a fall.
It is better to be of a lowly spirit with the poor
>   than to divide the spoil with the proud.
[She] who gives heed to the word will prosper,
>   and happy is [she] who trusts in the LORD.

PROVERBS 16:16-20, RSV

By humility and the fear of the LORD
Are riches and honor and life.

PROVERBS 22:4, NKJV

A greedy [woman] stirs up dissension,
>   but [she] who trusts in the LORD will prosper.

[She] who trusts in [herself] is a fool,
    but [she] who walks in wisdom is kept safe.

PROVERBS 28:25-26

A [woman's] pride will bring [her] low,
    but [she] who is lowly in spirit will obtain honor.

PROVERBS 29:23, RSV

Once more the humble will rejoice in the LORD;
    the needy will rejoice in the Holy One of Israel.

ISAIAH 29:19

At that time the disciples came to Jesus and asked, "Who
is the greatest in the kingdom of heaven?" He called a
little child and had him stand among them. And he said:
"I tell you the truth, unless you change and become like
little children, you will never enter the kingdom of
heaven. Therefore, whoever humbles himself like this
child is the greatest in the kingdom of heaven."

MATTHEW 18:1-4

But [she] who is greatest among you shall be your servant.
And whoever exalts [herself] will be humbled, and [she]
who humbles [herself] will be exalted.

MATTHEW 23:11-12, NKJV

"If you want to claim credit, claim it for God." What you say about yourself means nothing in God's work. It's what God says about you that makes the difference.

2 CORINTHIANS 10:17-18, MSG

But he gives us more grace. That is why Scripture says:
"God opposes the proud
but gives grace to the humble."

JAMES 4:6

I WILL CALM YOUR FEARS

Have you ever counted how many references there are to *fear* in Scripture? Three hundred and sixty-five (one for every day of the year!). As many times as God proclaimed, "Fear not..." it is obvious that fear is a major hindrance to the Christian life.

Why is it such a hindrance? Because *fear* is the opposite of *faith*. When we focus on our fear rather than having faith in God to deliver us from evil, we are much more likely to lose the battle for sexual and emotional integrity. How can we focus on what we know God will do when we think we are doomed? Such lack of faith says to God, "Even though you've carried me this far, you are probably going to fail me now, aren't you?"

—*Every Woman's Battle*

Yet if you devote your heart to him
    and stretch out your hands to him,
if you put away the sin that is in your hand
    and allow no evil to dwell in your tent,
then you will lift up your face without shame;
    you will stand firm and without fear.
You will surely forget your trouble,
    recalling it only as waters gone by.
Life will be brighter than noonday,
    and darkness will become like morning.
You will be secure, because there is hope;
    you will look about you and take your rest in safety.
You will lie down, with no one to make you afraid,
    and many will court your favor.

JOB 11:13-19

Even though I walk
    through the valley of the shadow of death,
I will fear no evil,
    for you are with me;
your rod and your staff,
    they comfort me.
You prepare a table before me
    in the presence of my enemies.
You anoint my head with oil;
    my cup overflows.

Surely goodness and love will follow me
    all the days of my life,
and I will dwell in the house of the LORD
    forever.

PSALM 23:4-6

Those who live in the shelter of the Most High
    will find rest in the shadow of the
        Almighty.
This I declare of the LORD:
    He alone is my refuge, my place of safety;
    he is my God, and I am trusting him.
For he will rescue you from every trap
    and protect you from the fatal plague.
He will shield you with his wings.
    He will shelter you with his feathers.
    His faithful promises are your armor and
        protection.
Do not be afraid of the terrors of the night,
    nor fear the dangers of the day,
nor dread the plague that stalks in darkness,
    nor the disaster that strikes at midday.

PSALM 91:1-6, NLT

For the waywardness of the simple will kill them,
    and the complacency of fools will destroy them;

but whoever listens to me will live in safety
and be at ease, without fear of harm.

PROVERBS 1:32-33

Fear of man will prove to be a snare,
but whoever trusts in the LORD is kept safe.

PROVERBS 29:25

You will keep in perfect peace all who trust in you,
whose thoughts are fixed on you!
Trust in the LORD always,
for the LORD GOD is the eternal Rock.

ISAIAH 26:3-4, NLT

And he said to his disciples, "Therefore I tell you,
do not be anxious about your life, what you shall
eat, nor about your body, what you shall put on.
For life is more than food, and the body more than
clothing. Consider the ravens: they neither sow nor
reap, they have neither storehouse nor barn, and yet
God feeds them. Of how much more value are you
than the birds! And which of you by being anxious
can add a cubit to his span of life? If then you are
not able to do as small a thing as that, why are you
anxious about the rest? Consider the lilies, how they

grow; they neither toil nor spin; yet I tell you, even
Solomon in all his glory was not arrayed like one
of these.

LUKE 12:22-27, RSV

So don't be afraid, little flock. For it gives your Father
great happiness to give you the Kingdom.

LUKE 12:32, NLT

So, dear [sisters], you have no obligations whatever
to your old sinful nature to do what it begs you to
do. For if you keep on following it you are lost and
will perish, but if through the power of the Holy
Spirit you crush it and its evil deeds, you shall live.
For all who are led by the Spirit of God are [children]
of God.

And so we should not be like cringing, fearful
slaves, but we should behave like God's very own
children, adopted into the bosom of his family, and
calling to him, "Father, Father." For his Holy Spirit
speaks to us deep in our hearts and tells us that we
really are God's children. And since we are his children,
we will share his treasures—for all God gives to his Son
Jesus is now ours too.

ROMANS 8:12-17, TLB

For God has not given us a spirit of fear, but of power and of love and of a sound mind.

2 TIMOTHY 1:7, NKJV

For
"[She] that would love life
and see good days,
let [her] keep [her] tongue from evil
and [her] lips from speaking guile;
let [her] turn away from evil and do right;
let [her] seek peace and pursue it.
For the eyes of the Lord are upon the righteous,
and his ears are open to their prayer.
But the face of the Lord is against those that do evil."

Now who is there to harm you if you are zealous for what is right? But even if you do suffer for righteousness' sake, you will be blessed.

1 PETER 3:10-14, RSV

I WILL HELP YOU FORGIVE THOSE WHO HURT YOU

If you are to find the life God wants for you, you must do one more thing—you must forgive. This may be the last thing you want to do, but it may be the very thing you need to do most.

—*Every Woman's Battle*

Good sense makes a [woman] slow to anger,
    and it is [her] glory to overlook an offense.

PROVERBS 19:11, RSV

Do not say, "I'll pay you back for this wrong!"
    Wait for the LORD, and he will deliver you.

PROVERBS 20:22

There is a saying, "Love your friends and hate your enemies." But I say: Love your enemies! Pray for those who
persecute you! In that way you will be acting as true
[daughters] of your Father in heaven. For he gives his sun-
light to both the evil and the good, and sends rain on the
just and on the unjust too.

MATTHEW 5:43-45, TLB

For if you forgive men their trespasses, your heavenly
Father will also forgive you.

MATTHEW 6:14, NKJV

Therefore I tell you, whatever you ask for in prayer,
believe that you have received it, and it will be yours. And
when you stand praying, if you hold anything against anyone, forgive him, so that your Father in heaven may forgive you your sins.

MARK 11:24-25

Love your enemies! Do good to them! Lend to them! And don't be concerned about the fact that they won't repay. Then your reward from heaven will be very great, and you will truly be acting as [children] of God: for he is kind to the unthankful and to those who are very wicked.

Try to show as much compassion as your Father does.

Never criticize or condemn—or it will all come back on you. Go easy on others; then they will do the same for you. For if you give, you will get! Your gift will return to you in full and overflowing measure, pressed down, shaken together to make room for more, and running over. Whatever measure you use to give—large or small— will be used to measure what is given back to you.

LUKE 6:35-38, TLB

Bless those who persecute you; bless and do not curse them. Rejoice with those who rejoice, weep with those who weep. Live in harmony with one another; do not be haughty, but associate with the lowly; never be conceited. Repay no one evil for evil, but take thought for what is noble in the sight of all. If possible, so far as it depends upon you, live peaceably with all. Beloved, never avenge yourselves, but leave it to the wrath of God; for it is written, "Vengeance is mine, I will repay, says the Lord." No, "if your enemy is hungry, feed him; if he is thirsty, give him drink; for by so doing you will heap burning coals upon his head." Do not be overcome by evil, but overcome evil with good.

ROMANS 12:14-21, RSV

Therefore, as God's chosen people, holy and dearly loved, clothe yourselves with compassion, kindness, humility, gentleness and patience. Bear with each other and forgive whatever grievances you may have against one another. Forgive as the Lord forgave you.

COLOSSIANS 3:12-13

I WILL HELP YOU FORGIVE YOURSELF

One day as I was beating myself up for yet another emotional affair, my best friend interrupted me with these sobering words: "Do you know what you are saying about the blood that Jesus shed for you when you refuse to forgive yourself for your past? You are saying that His blood wasn't good enough for you. It didn't have enough power to cleanse you." She was right. Underlying all of my self-pity was the belief that what Jesus did for me couldn't possibly be enough to rid me of my stain. I needed some special miracle to set me free, and until I got that miracle, I had to beat myself up as an act of penance.

If this rings true for you as well, then guess what? The Holy

Spirit is telling you the same thing He told me back then: *Jesus opened your prison door. It's up to you to walk out!*

—*Every Woman's Battle*

> Surely he has borne our griefs
> > and carried our sorrows;
> yet we esteemed him stricken,
> > smitten by God, and afflicted.
> But he was wounded for our transgressions,
> > he was bruised for our iniquities;
> upon him was the chastisement that made us whole,
> > and with his stripes we are healed.

ISAIAH 53:4-5, RSV

This is the message God has given us to pass on to you: that God is Light and in him is no darkness at all. So if we say we are his friends, but go on living in spiritual darkness and sin, we are lying. But if we are living in the light of God's presence, just as Christ does, then we have wonderful fellowship and joy with each other, and the blood of Jesus his Son cleanses us from every sin.

If we say that we have no sin, we are only fooling ourselves, and refusing to accept the truth. But if we confess our sins to him, he can be depended on to forgive us and to cleanse us from every wrong.

1 JOHN 1:5-9, TLB

This is the only way we'll know we're living truly, living in God's reality. It's also the way to shut down debilitating self-criticism, even when there is something to it. For God is greater than our worried hearts and knows more about us than we do ourselves.

1 JOHN 3:19-20, MSG

I promise to give you
beauty for ashes

My love language is gift giving, and so is my best friend's (see Gary Chapman's *Five Love Languages* for more on this concept). Over the past fifteen years, we've had great fun finding just the right gift, or the perfect card, or the sweetest sentiment to express our affinity for one another. But I confess, Lisa is much better at this than I am. I'm glad she doesn't keep score, or else I'd come out on the losing end. But I know even if I gave her a bale of hay for her birthday and a lump of coal for Christmas every year, she'd still love me. She'd probably even continue to knock herself out searching for the perfect sweater that goes great with my green eyes or those hilarious cards that really make my day, even if I couldn't reciprocate with an equivalent gesture.

Consider the incredible gifts that God continues giving us every day, in spite of the fact that the meager gifts we can offer Him really pale in comparison. But He doesn't compare at all. It doesn't matter to Him that our gifts don't come close to measuring up to the greatness of His. Even if all we have to offer is brokenness and strife, He is honored to receive it and gives us glorious riches in return. His extravagant gifts are always in style and can't be exchanged for anything more fitting to our needs and desires.

I WILL WASH YOU WHITE AS SNOW

Waving a white flag in the midst of battle is a symbol of surrender. A white flag symbolizes that the troops are no longer posting their own colors, but a neutral color as a sign of defeat. However, the white flag you will be waving as you surrender your past pain, present pride, and future fear is *not* a symbol of defeat. It is a symbol of victory, for it represents purity. You will be washed clean of all compromise as you allow God to transform you—your heart and mind—into a woman who forgives her debtors, walks in humility, and faces the future with confidence in her Creator and Sustainer.

White is your color, girlfriend! Post it proudly and enjoy the peacefulness and fulfillment of sweet surrender to the Savior.

—*Every Woman's Battle*

For the Lord your God is full of kindness and mercy and will not continue to turn away his face from you if you return to him.

2 CHRONICLES 30:9, TLB

Come now, let us reason together....
Though your sins are like scarlet,
    they shall be as white as snow;
though they are red as crimson,
    they shall be like wool.

ISAIAH 1:18

But I, yes I, am the one
    who takes care of your sins—that's what I do.
    I don't keep a list of your sins.

ISAIAH 43:25, MSG

Seek the LORD while he may be found;

    call on him while he is near.

Let the wicked forsake [her] way

    and the evil [woman her] thoughts.

Let [her] turn to the LORD, and he will have mercy

        on [her],

    and to our God, for he will freely pardon.

ISAIAH 55:6-7

I will sprinkle clean water upon you, and you shall be clean from all your uncleannesses, and from all your idols I will cleanse you. A new heart I will give you, and a new spirit I will put within you; and I will take out of your flesh the heart of stone and give you a heart of flesh. And I will put my spirit within you, and cause you to walk in my statutes and be careful to observe my ordinances. You shall dwell in the land which I gave to your fathers; and you shall be my people, and I will be your God.

EZEKIEL 36:25-28, RSV

Now the Lord is the Spirit, and where the Spirit of the Lord is, there is freedom. And we, who with unveiled faces all reflect the Lord's glory, are being transformed into his likeness with ever-increasing glory, which comes from the Lord, who is the Spirit.

2 CORINTHIANS 3:17-18

Therefore, if any one is in Christ, [she] is a new creation; the old has passed away, behold, the new has come.

2 CORINTHIANS 5:17, RSV

Because of the sacrifice of the Messiah, his blood poured out on the altar of the Cross, we're a free people—free of penalties and punishments chalked up by all our misdeeds. And not just barely free, either. Abundantly free!

EPHESIANS 1:7, MSG

It wasn't so long ago that we ourselves were stupid and stubborn, dupes of sin, ordered every which way by our glands, going around with a chip on our shoulder, hated and hating back. But when God, our kind and loving Savior God, stepped in, he saved us from all that. It was all his doing; we had nothing to do with it. He gave us a good bath, and we came out of it new people, washed inside and out by the Holy Spirit.

TITUS 3:3-5, MSG

But we know that when he appears, we shall be like him, for we shall see him as he is. Everyone who has this hope in him purifies himself, just as he is pure. Everyone

who sins breaks the law; in fact, sin is lawlessness. But
you know that he appeared so that he might take away
our sins.

1 JOHN 3:2-5

I WILL REMOVE YOUR SHAME

In my attempts to fill the father-shaped hole in my heart and estab-
lish some semblance of self-worth through these dysfunctional
relationships, I was creating a long list of shameful liaisons and a
trunk load of emotional baggage. I was overlooking the only true
source of satisfaction and self-worth: an intimate relationship with
my heavenly Father. Through pursuing this relationship first and
foremost, not only has Jesus become my first love and given me
a sense of worth beyond what any man could give, He has also
restored my relationship with my earthly father and helped me
remain faithful to my husband.

—*Every Woman's Battle*

Blessed are the undefiled in the way,
Who walk in the law of the LORD!
Blessed are those who keep His testimonies,
Who seek Him with the whole heart!
They also do no iniquity;

They walk in His ways.

You have commanded us

To keep Your precepts diligently.

Oh, that my ways were directed

To keep Your statutes!

Then I would not be ashamed,

When I look into all Your commandments.

I will praise You with uprightness of heart,

When I learn Your righteous judgments.

PSALM 119:1-7, NKJV

Do not fear, for you will not be ashamed;

Neither be disgraced, for you will not be put to shame;

For you will forget the shame of your youth,

And will not remember the reproach of your widowhood

anymore.

For your Maker is your husband,

The LORD of hosts is His name;

And your Redeemer is the Holy One of Israel;

He is called the God of the whole earth.

ISAIAH 54:4-5, NKJV

I have come into the world as a light, so that no one who believes in me should stay in darkness.

JOHN 12:46

As the Scripture says, "Anyone who trusts in him will never be put to shame."

ROMANS 10:11

But I am not ashamed, for I know whom I have believed, and I am sure that he is able to guard until that Day what has been entrusted to me.

2 TIMOTHY 1:12, RSV

Work hard so God can say to you, "Well done." Be a good workman, one who does not need to be ashamed when God examines your work. Know what his Word says and means.

2 TIMOTHY 2:15, TLB

For I will be merciful to their unrighteousness, and their sins and their lawless deeds I will remember no more.

HEBREWS 8:12, NKJV

I WILL GRANT YOU PEACE THAT PASSES UNDERSTANDING

I recently met a young woman who grew up in the war-torn country of Sierra Leone in West Africa. As bullets whizzed through the city streets and landmines blasted limbs off of children playing in the fields, every day was a struggle for Lela and her family to survive. She had been in the United States less than two years when I asked her what she liked most about living in this country.

She answered with a sweet smile, "Peace. There is nothing like living in peace."

I also asked, "How did you cope with the chaos of war all around you day after day?"

Shrugging her shoulders, she replied, "When war is all you have ever known, you don't realize how chaotic it is."

Although I've never known the terror of dodging bullets or landmines, the truth of Lela's statement struck a chord. I never realized how intense and chaotic my life was until I experienced the peace of living with sexual and emotional integrity.

—*Every Woman's Battle*

The fruit of righteousness will be peace;
> the effect of righteousness will be quietness
> > and confidence forever.
My people will live in peaceful dwelling places,
> in secure homes,
> in undisturbed places of rest.

ISAIAH 32:17-18

"Peace, peace, to those far and near,"
> says the LORD. "And I will heal them."

ISAIAH 57:19

And Jesus said to the woman, "Your faith has saved you; go in peace."

LUKE 7:50, TLB

Peace I leave with you; my peace I give to you; not as the world gives do I give to you. Let not your hearts be troubled, neither let them be afraid.

JOHN 14:27, RSV

Rejoice in the Lord always; again I will say, Rejoice. Let all men know your forbearance. The Lord is at hand. Have no anxiety about anything, but in everything by prayer and supplication with thanksgiving let your requests be made known to God. And the peace of God, which passes all understanding, will keep your hearts and your minds in Christ Jesus.

PHILIPPIANS 4:4-7, RSV

Let the peace of Christ rule in your hearts, since as members of one body you were called to peace. And be thankful. Let the word of Christ dwell in you richly as you teach and admonish one another with all wisdom, and as you sing psalms, hymns and spiritual songs with gratitude in your hearts to God. And whatever you do, whether in word or deed, do it all in the name of the Lord Jesus, giving thanks to God the Father through him.

COLOSSIANS 3:15-17

Now may the Lord of peace Himself give you
peace always in every way. The Lord be with
you all.

2 Thessalonians 3:16, nkjv

WHEN YOU DELIGHT YOURSELF IN ME, I WILL BLESS YOU WITH JOY UNSPEAKABLE

Oh, how Jesus longs for His own to acknowledge Him, to introduce Him to our friends, to withdraw to be alone with Him, to cling to Him for our identity, to gaze longingly into His eyes, to love Him with all our heart and soul.

What about you? Do you have this kind of love relationship with Christ? Do you experience the inexplicable joy of intimacy with the one who loves you with a passion far deeper, far greater than anything you could find here on earth? I know from experience that you can.

—*Every Woman's Battle*

Do not grieve, for the joy of the LORD is your
strength.

Nehemiah 8:10

Our soul waits for the LORD;
He is our help and our shield.

For our heart shall rejoice in Him,
Because we have trusted in His holy name.

PSALM 33:20-21, NKJV

O God, my God! How I search for you! How I thirst for
you in this parched and weary land where there is no water.
How I long to find you! How I wish I could go into your
sanctuary to see your strength and glory, for your love and
kindness are better to me than life itself. How I praise you!
I will bless you as long as I live, lifting up my hands to you
in prayer. At last I shall be fully satisfied; I will praise you
with great joy. I lie awake at night thinking of you—of how
much you have helped me—and how I rejoice through the
night beneath the protecting shadow of your wings.

PSALM 63:1-7, TLB

The godly will rejoice in the LORD
        and find shelter in him.
And those who do what is right
        will praise him.

PSALM 64:10, NLT

But may the righteous be glad
        and rejoice before God;
        may they be happy and joyful.

PSALM 68:3

Blessed are the people who know the joyful sound!
They walk, O Lord, in the light of Your countenance.
In Your name they rejoice all day long,
And in Your righteousness they are exalted.

PSALM 89:15-16, NKJV

I was pushed back and about to fall,
        but the Lord helped me.
The Lord is my strength and my song;
        he has become my salvation.
Shouts of joy and victory
        resound in the tents of the righteous:
"The Lord's right hand has done mighty things!"

PSALM 118:13-15

The ransomed of the Lord will return.
        They will enter Zion with singing;
        everlasting joy will crown their heads.
Gladness and joy will overtake them,
        and sorrow and sighing will flee away.

ISAIAH 51:11

You will go out in joy
        and be led forth in peace;
the mountains and hills
        will burst into song before you,

and all the trees of the field
will clap their hands.

ISAIAH 55:12

I have loved you even as the Father has loved me. Live
within my love. When you obey me you are living in my
love, just as I obey my Father and live in his love. I have
told you this so that you will be filled with my joy. Yes,
your cup of joy will overflow!

JOHN 15:9-11, TLB

So you have sorrow now, but I will see you again and your
hearts will rejoice, and no one will take your joy from you.

JOHN 16:22, RSV

You love him even though you have never seen him;
though not seeing him, you trust him; and even now you
are happy with the inexpressible joy that comes from
heaven itself.

1 PETER 1:8, TLB

I PROMISE TO GIVE YOU EVERLASTING HOPE

If you've already run the red light, please know there is hope for
you. I've known many women who have journeyed to this depth of

desperation, hoping to find something to fill the void in their hearts, only to discover that the pit was far deeper, darker, and more lonely than they could have imagined. I'm one of those women, but after many years of focusing my attentions and affections on my first love (Jesus Christ) and my second love (my husband), my life is a testimony to God's changing grace. In His lavish love, God's arm of mercy reaches further than we could ever fall.

—*Every Woman's Battle*

O LORD, you alone are my hope; I've trusted you from childhood. Yes, you have been with me from birth and have helped me constantly—no wonder I am always praising you! My success—at which so many stand amazed—is because you are my mighty protector. All day long I'll praise and honor you, O God, for all that you have done for me.

PSALM 71:5-8, TLB

The wicked is overthrown through [her] evil-doing,
    but the righteous finds refuge through [her] integrity.

PROVERBS 14:32, RSV

Therefore, since we have been made right in God's sight by faith, we have peace with God because of what Jesus Christ our Lord has done for us. Because of our faith,

Christ has brought us into this place of highest privilege where we now stand, and we confidently and joyfully look forward to sharing God's glory.

We can rejoice, too, when we run into problems and trials, for we know that they are good for us—they help us learn to endure. And endurance develops strength of character in us, and character strengthens our confident expectation of salvation. And this expectation will not disappoint us. For we know how dearly God loves us, because he has given us the Holy Spirit to fill our hearts with his love.

Romans 5:1-5, nlt

May our Lord Jesus Christ himself and God our Father, who loved us and by his grace gave us eternal encouragement and good hope, encourage your hearts and strengthen you in every good deed and word.

2 Thessalonians 2:16-17

Praise be to the God and Father of our Lord Jesus Christ! In his great mercy he has given us new birth into a living hope through the resurrection of Jesus Christ from the dead, and into an inheritance that can never perish, spoil or fade—kept in heaven for you, who through faith are shielded by God's power until the coming of the salvation that is ready to be revealed in the last time....

Through him you believe in God, who raised him
from the dead and glorified him, and so your faith and
hope are in God.

1 Peter 1: 3-5,21

I promise
to show you My ways

I promise
to show you my ways

One of the first nicknames my mother ever gave me was "Little Miss Independent." I liked to do things my way, even if it took twice as long and required twice as much effort.

This character trait has followed me throughout life and has served me well at times, but it's been a real hindrance at others. It's especially been a challenge for my husband, who doesn't appreciate my telling him exactly how he should be doing something when his way is quite acceptable. I've had to accept the fact that my way isn't always the best way and is certainly not the only way!

This is especially true when it comes to my pursuit of sexual and emotional fulfillment. For years, I tried to create intimacy and discover relational satisfaction my own way, but to say that these ways were a hindrance is a gross understatement. I almost lost the most precious relationships I could ever experience—those with my own family. I had to surrender my ways when it became evident that they weren't working but rather were working against me.

I had to adopt God's way of pursuing sexual and emotional fulfillment. Rather than living up to my "Little Miss Independent" reputation, I've had to learn to be "Little Miss Dependent" on God. In my dependence upon God's ways, I've found a deeper level of satisfaction than I ever could have manufactured doing things my way.

I WILL REVEAL TRUTH TO YOU

To help us guard against temptation, Paul encourages Christians to put on the "full armor of God"—the belt of truth, the breastplate of righteousness, shoes of peace, the shield of faith, the helmet of salvation, and the sword of the Spirit (see Ephesians 6:13-17). We are so fortunate that the Holy Spirit gives us complete access to all of these things since truth, righteousness, peace, and faith are key ingredients to maintaining sexual and emotional integrity.

—*Every Woman's Battle*

I will bless the LORD who has given me counsel;
My heart also instructs me in the night seasons.
I have set the LORD always before me;
Because He is at my right hand I shall not be moved.

PSALM 16:7-8, NKJV

You are my hiding place from every storm of life; you
even keep me from getting into trouble! You surround me
with songs of victory. I will instruct you (says the Lord)
and guide you along the best pathway for your life; I will
advise you and watch your progress.

PSALM 32:7-8, TLB

My [daughter], if you receive my words
        and treasure up my commandments with you,
making your ear attentive to wisdom
        and inclining your heart to understanding;
yes, if you cry out for insight
        and raise your voice for understanding,

if you seek it like silver
    and search for it as for hidden treasures;
then you will understand the fear of the LORD
    and find the knowledge of God.
For the LORD gives wisdom;
    from his mouth come knowledge and understanding;
he stores up sound wisdom for the upright;
    he is a shield to those who walk in integrity,
guarding the paths of justice
    and preserving the way of his saints.

PROVERBS 2:1-8, RSV

To the [woman] who pleases him, God gives wisdom, knowledge and happiness.

ECCLESIASTES 2:26

He will not stop until truth and righteousness prevail throughout the earth. Even distant lands beyond the sea will wait for his instruction.

ISAIAH 42:4, NLT

Jesus said to the people who believed in him, "You are truly my disciples if you keep obeying my teachings. And you will know the truth, and the truth will set you free."

JOHN 8:31-32, NLT

If you love me, you will keep my commandments. And I
will pray the Father, and he will give you another Counselor, to be with you for ever, even the Spirit of truth,
whom the world cannot receive, because it neither sees
him nor knows him; you know him, for he dwells with
you, and will be in you.

JOHN 14:15-17, RSV

When the Spirit of truth comes, he will guide you into all
truth. He will not be presenting his own ideas; he will be telling you what he has heard. He will tell you about the future.

JOHN 16:13, NLT

If any of you lacks wisdom, let [her] ask of God, who
gives to all liberally and without reproach, and it will be
given to [her]. But let [her] ask in faith, with no doubting,
for [she] who doubts is like a wave of the sea driven and
tossed by the wind.

JAMES 1:5-6, NKJV

BECAUSE MY WAYS ARE MERCIFUL, I WILL NEVER HOLD YOUR PAST AGAINST YOU

When I am justified, it is "*just as if I'd* never done those things."
So why do we continue beating ourselves up? Why do we allow

our misery to affect our mental and physical health? You don't have to carry all that emotional baggage. Surrender your pain and your backpack full of guilt and shame; it is only making you tired and crabby. Travel light and let the joy of the Lord be your strength!

—*Every Woman's Battle*

Show me your ways, O LORD,
    teach me your paths;
guide me in your truth and teach me,
    for you are God my Savior,
    and my hope is in you all day long.
Remember, O LORD, your great mercy
        and love,
    for they are from of old.
Remember not the sins of my youth
    and my rebellious ways;
according to your love remember me,
    for you are good, O LORD.

PSALM 25:4-7

For his anger lasts only a moment,
    but his favor lasts a lifetime;
weeping may remain for a night,
    but rejoicing comes in the morning.

PSALM 30:5

He is merciful and tender toward those who don't deserve it; he is slow to get angry and full of kindness and love. He never bears a grudge, nor remains angry forever. He has not punished us as we deserve for all our sins, for his mercy toward those who fear and honor him is as great as the height of the heavens above the earth. He has removed our sins as far away from us as the east is from the west. He is like a father to us, tender and sympathetic to those who reverence him. For he knows we are but dust and that our days are few and brief, like grass, like flowers, blown by the wind and gone forever.

But the lovingkindness of the Lord is from everlasting to everlasting, to those who reverence him; his salvation is to children's children of those who are faithful to his covenant and remember to obey him!

PSALM 103:8-18, TLB

But to all who received him, who believed in his name, he gave power to become children of God.

JOHN 1:12, RSV

And all the prophets have written about him, saying that everyone who believes in him will have their sins forgiven through his name.

ACTS 10:43, TLB

And you, being dead in your trespasses and the uncircum-
cision of your flesh, He has made alive together with Him,
having forgiven you all trespasses, having wiped out the
handwriting of requirements that was against us, which
was contrary to us. And He has taken it out of the way,
having nailed it to the cross.

COLOSSIANS 2:13-14, NKJV

I am writing these things to all of you, my little children,
because your sins have been forgiven in the name of Jesus
our Savior.

1 JOHN 2:12, TLB

I WILL TEACH YOU HEALTHY WAYS
TO LOVE OTHERS

We are each held accountable by God for what we know to do. If
we want to gain the prize of sexual integrity, we may need to let go
of some of our "freedoms" (in dress, thoughts, speech, and behav-
ior) in order to serve the best interest of others out of love. God
will not only provide this knowledge of how to act with integrity, He
will also honor those who apply this knowledge and act with
responsibility.

—*Every Woman's Battle*

And so I am giving a new commandment to you now—
love each other just as much as I love you. Your strong
love for each other will prove to the world that you are
my disciples.

JOHN 13:34-35, TLB

Love must be sincere. Hate what is evil; cling to what is
good. Be devoted to one another in brotherly love. Honor
one another above yourselves. Never be lacking in zeal,
but keep your spiritual fervor, serving the Lord. Be joyful
in hope, patient in affliction, faithful in prayer. Share with
God's people who are in need. Practice hospitality.

Bless those who persecute you; bless and do not curse.
Rejoice with those who rejoice; mourn with those who
mourn. Live in harmony with one another. Do not be
proud, but be willing to associate with people of low posi-
tion. Do not be conceited.

Do not repay anyone evil for evil. Be careful to do
what is right in the eyes of everybody. If it is possible, as
far as it depends on you, live at peace with everyone.

ROMANS 12:9-18

Love is patient, love is kind. It does not envy, it does not
boast, it is not proud. It is not rude, it is not self-seeking, it
is not easily angered, it keeps no record of wrongs. Love

does not delight in evil but rejoices with the truth. It always
protects, always trusts, always hopes, always perseveres.

1 CORINTHIANS 13:4-7

But if instead of showing love among yourselves you are
always biting and devouring one another, watch out!
Beware of destroying one another.

So I advise you to live according to your new life in
the Holy Spirit. Then you won't be doing what your sinful nature craves. The old sinful nature loves to do evil,
which is just opposite from what the Holy Spirit wants.
And the Spirit gives us desires that are opposite from what
the sinful nature desires. These two forces are constantly
fighting each other, and your choices are never free from
this conflict.

GALATIANS 5:15-17, NLT

It is obvious what kind of life develops out of trying to get
your own way all the time: repetitive, loveless, cheap sex; a
stinking accumulation of mental and emotional garbage;
frenzied and joyless grabs for happiness; trinket gods;
magic-show religion; paranoid loneliness; cutthroat com-
petition; all-consuming-yet-never-satisfied wants; a brutal
temper; an impotence to love or be loved; divided homes
and divided lives; small-minded and lopsided pursuits; the

vicious habit of depersonalizing everyone into a rival;
uncontrolled and uncontrollable addictions; ugly parodies
of community. I could go on.

This isn't the first time I have warned you, you know.
If you use your freedom this way, you will not inherit
God's kingdom.

GALATIANS 5:19-21, MSG

Finally, brethren, whatever is true, whatever is honorable,
whatever is just, whatever is pure, whatever is lovely, whatever is gracious, if there is any excellence, if there is anything worthy of praise, think about these things. What
you have learned and received and heard and seen in me,
do; and the God of peace will be with you.

PHILIPPIANS 4:8-9, RSV

Do not participate in the sins of others. Keep yourself pure.

1 TIMOTHY 5:22, NLT

Now that you have purified yourselves by obeying the
truth so that you have sincere love for your brothers, love
one another deeply, from the heart. For you have been
born again, not of perishable seed, but of imperishable,
through the living and enduring word of God.

1 PETER 1:22-23

So make every effort to apply the benefits of these promises to your life. Then your faith will produce a life of moral excellence. A life of moral excellence leads to knowing God better. Knowing God leads to self-control. Self-control leads to patient endurance, and patient endurance leads to godliness. Godliness leads to love for other Christians, and finally you will grow to have genuine love for everyone. The more you grow like this, the more you will become productive and useful in your knowledge of our Lord Jesus Christ.

2 PETER 1:5-8, NLT

Beloved, let us love one another, for love is of God; and everyone who loves is born of God and knows God. He who does not love does not know God, for God is love. In this the love of God was manifested toward us, that God has sent His only begotten Son into the world, that we might live through Him. In this is love, not that we loved God, but that He loved us and sent His Son to be the propitiation for our sins. Beloved, if God so loved us, we also ought to love one another.

No one has seen God at any time. If we love one another, God abides in us, and His love has been perfected in us.

1 JOHN 4:7-12, NKJV

MY WORD WILL TEACH YOU AND GUIDE YOU

Either sin will keep you from the Bible, or the Bible will keep you from sin.

Of course, reading or even studying the Bible won't keep you from sin. (Just look at all the pastors who are Bible scholars yet have engaged in sexual sin.) We have to *internalize* and *apply* what the Bible says.... Your mind can only concentrate on so many things at once, and the more you concentrate on wholesome thoughts, the more your unwholesome thoughts will have to take a back seat.

—*Every Woman's Battle*

Place these words on your hearts. Get them deep inside you. Tie them on your hands and foreheads as a reminder. Teach them to your children. Talk about them wherever you are, sitting at home or walking in the street; talk about them from the time you get up in the morning until you fall into bed at night. Inscribe them on the doorposts and gates of your cities so that you'll live a long time, and your children with you, on the soil that GOD promised to give your ancestors for as long as there is a sky over the Earth.

DEUTERONOMY 11:18-21, MSG

Be vigilant, listen obediently to these words that I command you so that you'll have a good life, you and your

children, for a long, long time, doing what is good and
right in the eyes of GOD, your God.

DEUTERONOMY 12:28, MSG

Be strong and very courageous. Be careful to obey all the
law my servant Moses gave you; do not turn from it to
the right or to the left, that you may be successful wherever you go. Do not let this Book of the Law depart from
your mouth; meditate on it day and night, so that you
may be careful to do everything written in it. Then you
will be prosperous and successful.

JOSHUA 1:7-8

As for God, his way is perfect.
All the LORD's promises prove true.
He is a shield for all who look to him for protection.

2 SAMUEL 22:31, NLT

Forever, O Lord, your Word stands firm in heaven. Your
faithfulness extends to every generation, like the earth you
created; it endures by your decree, for everything serves
your plans.

I would have despaired and perished unless your
laws had been my deepest delight. I will never lay aside
your laws, for you have used them to restore my joy
and health. I am yours! Save me! For I have tried to live

according to your desires. Though the wicked hide along the way to kill me, I will quietly keep my mind upon your promises.

Nothing is perfect except your words. Oh, how I love them. I think about them all day long. They make me wiser than my enemies, because they are my constant guide. Yes, wiser than my teachers, for I am ever thinking of your rules. They make me even wiser than the aged.

PSALM 119:89-100, TLB

Your word is a lamp for my feet
    and a light for my path.
I've promised it once, and I'll promise again:
    I will obey your wonderful laws.

PSALM 119:105-106, NLT

Thy testimonies are wonderful;
    therefore my soul keeps them.
The unfolding of thy words gives light;
    it imparts understanding to the simple.
With open mouth I pant,
    because I long for thy commandments.

PSALM 119:129-131, RSV

See how I love your precepts;
    preserve my life, O LORD, according to your love.

All your words are true;

all your righteous laws are eternal.

PSALM 119:159-160

And now I entrust you to God and his care and to his wonderful words that are able to build your faith and give you
all the inheritance of those who are set apart for himself.

ACTS 20:32, TLB

I am not ashamed of the gospel, because it is the power
of God for the salvation of everyone who believes: first
for the Jew, then for the Gentile. For in the gospel a righteousness from God is revealed, a righteousness that is by
faith from first to last, just as it is written: "The righteous
will live by faith."

ROMANS 1:16-17

Consequently, faith comes from hearing the message, and
the message is heard through the word of Christ.

ROMANS 10:17

There's nothing like the written Word of God for showing you the way to salvation through faith in Christ Jesus.
Every part of Scripture is God-breathed and useful one
way or another—showing us truth, exposing our rebellion, correcting our mistakes, training us to live God's

way. Through the Word we are put together and shaped up for the tasks God has for us.

2 TIMOTHY 3:15-17, MSG

For the word of God is living and powerful, and sharper than any two-edged sword, piercing even to the division of soul and spirit, and of joints and marrow, and is a discerner of the thoughts and intents of the heart.

HEBREWS 4:12, NKJV

So get rid of all the filth and evil in your lives, and humbly accept the message God has planted in your hearts, for it is strong enough to save your souls.

And remember, it is a message to obey, not just to listen to. If you don't obey, you are only fooling yourself. For if you just listen and don't obey, it is like looking at your face in a mirror but doing nothing to improve your appearance. You see yourself, walk away, and forget what you look like. But if you keep looking steadily into God's perfect law—the law that sets you free—and if you do what it says and don't forget what you heard, then God will bless you for doing it.

JAMES 1:21-25, NLT

You have been born anew, not of perishable seed but of imperishable, through the living and abiding word of God; for

"All flesh is like grass
  and all its glory like the flower of grass.
The grass withers, and the flower falls,
  but the word of the Lord abides for
     ever."

1 PETER 1:23-25, RSV

I PROMISE I HAVE A PLAN FOR YOUR LIFE

Taking one day at a time and trusting our future to God *is* all it takes [to remain faithful]. That's why Jesus taught us to pray, "Give us this day, our daily bread." That is why God rained down bread from heaven each day when the Israelites were wandering in the desert without food—so that His people would learn *daily* dependence on Him. When we change our focus from the distant future to the immediate present, we gain the strength and courage to overcome the fear of what we may encounter down the road. Don't focus on whether you can be faithful to one man for a lifetime— just focus on being faithful to him (or to God if you are single) just for today. Then do the same thing tomorrow, and the next day, and the next.

—*Every Woman's Battle*

O LORD, you are my God;
  I will exalt you and praise your name,

for in perfect faithfulness

> you have done marvelous things,

> things planned long ago.

ISAIAH 25:1

Therefore whoever hears these sayings of Mine, and does them, I will liken [her] to a wise [woman] who built [her] house on the rock: and the rain descended, the floods came, and the winds blew and beat on that house; and it did not fall, for it was founded on the rock.

But everyone who hears these sayings of Mine, and does not do them, will be like a foolish [woman] who built [her] house on the sand: and the rain descended, the floods came, and the winds blew and beat on that house; and it fell. And great was its fall.

MATTHEW 7:24-27, NKJV

And we know that in all things God works for the good of those who love him, who have been called according to his purpose. For those God foreknew he also predestined to be conformed to the likeness of his Son, that he might be the firstborn among many brothers. And those he predestined, he also called; those he called, he also justified; those he justified, he also glorified.

What, then, shall we say in response to this? If God is for us, who can be against us?

ROMANS 8:28-31

But, as it is written,

"What no eye has seen, nor ear heard,
nor the heart of [woman] conceived,
what God has prepared for those who love him."

1 CORINTHIANS 2:9, RSV

Don't be misled; remember that you can't ignore God and get away with it: a [woman] will always reap just the kind of crop [she] sows! If [she] sows to please [her] own wrong desires, [she] will be planting seeds of evil and [she] will surely reap a harvest of spiritual decay and death; but if [she] plants the good things of the Spirit, [she] will reap the everlasting life that the Holy Spirit gives [her]. And let us not get tired of doing what is right, for after a while we will reap a harvest of blessing if we don't get discouraged and give up.

GALATIANS 6:7-9, TLB

I promise to reward
your obedience

As humans, we are often driven by rewards. We strive to impress people because of the accolades we hope to receive. We work hard to earn a good paycheck and to move up the corporate ladder. We even fly with a certain airline, even if it costs a little more, because we can earn frequent-flyer rewards. It's in our nature to seek rewards.

When I was "looking for love in all the wrong places," I perceived that there were rewards to turning a stranger's head with my flattering curves or making a guy's eyes pop out of his head with a flirty innuendo. I liked to feel good about my sex appeal, and I didn't think I was hurting anyone. But God showed me that I was hurting others, causing my brothers to stumble and fall into temptation, not to mention often causing myself to stumble and fall as well. I was actually missing out on much greater rewards.

Feeling good about what we look like pales in comparison to feeling good about who we really are, both inside and out. When we act with integrity, we not only reap the personal intrinsic rewards of dignity and self-respect, but we also reap the many generous rewards God has for those whose walk is honoring to Him.

IF YOU OBEY ME, I WILL GIVE YOU A BRIGHT FUTURE

I never realized how intense and chaotic my life was until I experienced the peace of living with sexual and emotional integrity. For years I had walked blindly into compromising situations, begged over dinner tables for morsels of affection, and found myself sleeping with the enemy time and time again. I consistently mistook intensity for intimacy and the concept of a peaceful relationship seemed unfathomable.

But God, in His sovereignty, looked beyond my weaknesses and saw my need for genuine intimacy. And in spite of my unfaithfulness, He's been faithful to guide me toward that place of quiet rest in my relationships with my father, my husband, and myself.

—*Every Woman's Battle*

Oh, that they had such a heart in them that they would fear Me and always keep all My commandments, that it might be well with them and with their children forever!

DEUTERONOMY 5:29, NKJV

You shall diligently keep the commandments of the LORD your God, and his testimonies, and his statutes, which he has commanded you. And you shall do what is right and good in the sight of the LORD, that it may go well with you, and that you may go in and take possession of the good land which the LORD swore to give to your fathers.

DEUTERONOMY 6:17-18, RSV

Carefully follow the terms of this covenant, so that you may prosper in everything you do.

DEUTERONOMY 29:9

Consider the blameless, observe the upright;

there is a future for the [woman] of peace.

PSALM 37:37

When a [woman's] ways are pleasing to the LORD,

he makes even [her] enemies live at peace with [her].

Better a little with righteousness

than much gain with injustice.

In [her] heart a [woman] plans [her] course,

but the LORD determines [her] steps.

PROVERBS 16:7-9

And the LORD will guide you continually,

and satisfy your desire with good things,

and make your bones strong;

and you shall be like a watered garden,

like a spring of water,

whose waters fail not.

ISAIAH 58:11, RSV

Because of the LORD's great love we are not consumed,

for his compassions never fail.

They are new every morning;

great is your faithfulness.

I say to myself, "The LORD is my portion;

therefore I will wait for him."

The LORD is good to those whose hope is in him,

to the one who seeks him;

it is good to wait quietly

for the salvation of the LORD.

LAMENTATIONS 3:22-26

Now we have received not the spirit of the world, but the Spirit which is from God, that we might understand the gifts bestowed on us by God.

1 CORINTHIANS 2:12, RSV

IF YOU REMAIN IN ME, I WILL GIVE YOU A FRUITFUL LIFE

Perhaps some people might think you are legalistic [because you are more discerning about what you watch or listen to and where you go]....

But you know what will be evident in your life? You are a woman of conviction, and you live by those convictions. Others will see that your actions back up your words and that you give careful thought to the kind of woman you want to be. And if they ever come to realize that their lifestyles are not bringing them the fulfillment they long for, guess who they will likely run to for wise counsel? You guessed it: the woman who they know can teach them how to take every thought captive and live the overcoming life!

—*Every Woman's Battle*

Oh, the joys of those
>   who do not follow the advice of the wicked,
>   or stand around with sinners,
>   or join in with scoffers.
But they delight in doing everything the LORD wants;
>   day and night they think about his law.
They are like trees planted along the riverbank,
>   bearing fruit each season without fail.
Their leaves never wither,
>   and in all they do, they prosper.

PSALM 1:1-3, NLT

The righteous will flourish like a palm tree,
>   they will grow like a cedar of Lebanon;
planted in the house of the LORD,
>   they will flourish in the courts of our God.
They will still bear fruit in old age,
>   they will stay fresh and green,
proclaiming, "The LORD is upright;
>   he is my Rock, and there is no wickedness
>   in him."

PSALM 92:12-15

Say to the righteous that it shall be well with them,
For they shall eat the fruit of their doings.

ISAIAH 3:10, NKJV

Sow for yourselves righteousness,

    reap the fruit of steadfast love;

break up your fallow ground,

    for it is the time to seek the LORD,

    that he may come and rain salvation upon you.

HOSEA 10:12, RSV

All this is from God, who through Christ reconciled us to himself and gave us the ministry of reconciliation; that is, in Christ God was reconciling the world to himself, not counting their trespasses against them, and entrusting to us the message of reconciliation. So we are ambassadors for Christ, God making his appeal through us. We beseech you on behalf of Christ, be reconciled to God. For our sake he made him to be sin who knew no sin, so that in him we might become the righteousness of God.

2 CORINTHIANS 5:18-21, RSV

But what happens when we live God's way? He brings gifts into our lives, much the same way that fruit appears in an orchard—things like affection for others, exuberance about life, serenity. We develop a willingness to stick with things, a sense of compassion in the heart, and a conviction that a basic holiness permeates things and people. We find ourselves involved in loyal commitments, not need-

ing to force our way in life, able to marshal and direct our
energies wisely.

GALATIANS 5:22-23, MSG

We always thank God, the Father of our Lord Jesus Christ,
when we pray for you, because we have heard of your faith
in Christ Jesus and of the love you have for all the saints—
the faith and love that spring from the hope that is stored
up for you in heaven and that you have already heard about
in the word of truth, the gospel that has come to you. All
over the world this gospel is bearing fruit and growing, just
as it has been doing among you since the day you heard it
and understood God's grace in all its truth.

COLOSSIANS 1:3-6

I am the true vine, and my Father is the vinedresser. Every
branch of mine that bears no fruit, he takes away, and
every branch that does bear fruit he prunes, that it may
bear more fruit. You are already made clean by the word
which I have spoken to you. Abide in me, and I in you.
As the branch cannot bear fruit by itself, unless it abides
in the vine, neither can you, unless you abide in me. I am
the vine, you are the branches. He who abides in me, and
I in him, he it is that bears much fruit, for apart from me
you can do nothing.

JOHN 15:1-5, RSV

Endure hardship as discipline; God is treating you as
[daughters]. For what [daughter] is not disciplined by
[her] father? If you are not disciplined (and everyone
undergoes discipline), then you are illegitimate children
and not true [daughters]. Moreover, we have all had
human fathers who disciplined us and we respected them
for it. How much more should we submit to the Father of
our spirits and live! Our fathers disciplined us for a little
while as they thought best; but God disciplines us for our
good, that we may share in his holiness. No discipline
seems pleasant at the time, but painful. Later on, however,
it produces a harvest of righteousness and peace for those
who have been trained by it.

HEBREWS 12:7-11

I HAVE RICH REWARDS AWAITING YOU

My joy isn't this land or a ministry or even restored self-esteem.
My very great reward is all of the intimacies and ecstasies that I
experience with the Lord Himself, a relationship that fills me to
overflowing, gives me unspeakable joy, and causes all other relationships to pale in comparison.

I'm not promising that God will give you the same physical
rewards I received. However, I can promise that He longs to enjoy

this kind of intimate relationship with *you*. He also has rewards custom-tailored just for you that will delight your heart the way He has delighted mine. He promises in Matthew 6:33 that if we seek first His kingdom and His righteousness that His blessings will be added to us as well.

—*Every Woman's Battle*

I am your shield,
> your very great reward.

GENESIS 15:1

But let all those rejoice who put their trust in You;
Let them ever shout for joy, because You defend them;
Let those also who love Your name
Be joyful in You.
For You, O LORD, will bless the righteous;
With favor You will surround [her] as with a shield.

PSALM 5:11-12, NKJV

Better is one day in your courts
> than a thousand elsewhere;
I would rather be a doorkeeper in the house of my God
> than dwell in the tents of the wicked.
For the LORD God is a sun and shield;
> the LORD bestows favor and honor;

no good thing does he withhold
> from those whose walk is blameless.

PSALM 84:10-11

You will eat the fruit of your labor;
> blessings and prosperity will be yours.

PSALM 128:2

Happy is the person who finds wisdom and gains understanding. For the profit of wisdom is better than silver,
and her wages are better than gold. Wisdom is more precious than rubies; nothing you desire can compare with
her. She offers you life in her right hand, and riches and
honor in her left. She will guide you down delightful
paths; all her ways are satisfying. Wisdom is a tree of life
to those who embrace her; happy are those who hold her
tightly.

PROVERBS 3:13-18, NLT

Misfortune pursues the sinner,
> but prosperity is the reward of the righteous.

PROVERBS 13:21

After looking at the way things are on this earth, here's
what I've decided is the best way to live: Take care of
yourself, have a good time, and make the most of what-

ever job you have for as long as God gives you life. And
that's about it. That's the human lot. Yes, we should make
the most of what God gives, both the bounty and the
capacity to enjoy it, accepting what's given and delighting
in the work. It's God's gift!

ECCLESIASTES 5:18-19, MSG

I the LORD search the heart
    and examine the mind,
to reward a [woman] according to [her] conduct,
    according to what [her] deeds deserve.

JEREMIAH 17:10

Blessed are the pure in heart,
    for they will see God.

MATTHEW 5:8

Everyone who has left houses or brothers or sisters or father
or mother or children or fields for my sake will receive a
hundred times as much and will inherit eternal life.

MATTHEW 19:29

And God is able to make all grace abound to you, so that
in all things at all times, having all that you need, you will
abound in every good work.

2 CORINTHIANS 9:8

Without faith it is impossible to please God, because anyone who comes to him must believe that he exists and
that he rewards those who earnestly seek him.

HEBREWS 11:6

All these people were still living by faith when they died.
They did not receive the things promised; they only saw
them and welcomed them from a distance. And they
admitted that they were aliens and strangers on earth.
People who say such things show that they are looking
for a country of their own. If they had been thinking of
the country they had left, they would have had opportu-
nity to return. Instead, they were longing for a better
country—a heavenly one. Therefore God is not ashamed
to be called their God, for he has prepared a city for
them.

HEBREWS 11:13-16

Blessed is the [woman] who endures trial, for when [she]
has stood the test [she] will receive the crown of life which
God has promised to those who love him.

JAMES 1:12, RSV

Do not be deceived.... Every good endowment and every
perfect gift is from above, coming down from the Father

of lights with whom there is no variation or shadow due to change. Of his own will he brought us forth by the word of truth that we should be a kind of first fruits of his creatures.

JAMES 1:16-18, RSV

Behold, I am coming soon! My reward is with me, and I will give to everyone according to what [she] has done.

REVELATION 22:12

I PROMISE YOU WILL FIND FULFILLMENT IN ETERNITY WITH ME

In our quest for relational intimacy, remember there is Someone we can whisper our heart's desires to and get our boosts from who isn't going to jeopardize our integrity but will strengthen it.

If you are thinking, *No way will talking to God ever excite me like talking to a man,* then you haven't allowed yourself to be courted by our Creator. The same God whose words possessed the power to form the entire universe longs to whisper into your hungry heart words that have the power to thrill you, heal you, and draw you into a deeper love relationship than you ever imagined possible.

—*Every Woman's Battle*

Jesus answered, "Everyone who drinks this water will be thirsty again, but whoever drinks the water I give [her] will never thirst. Indeed, the water I give [her] will become in [her] a spring of water welling up to eternal life."

JOHN 4:13-14

Jesus replied, "I am the Bread of Life. No one coming to me will ever be hungry again. Those believing in me will never thirst. But the trouble is, as I have told you before, you haven't believed even though you have seen me. But some will come to me—those the Father has given me—and I will never, never reject them. For I have come here from heaven to do the will of God who sent me, not to have my own way. And this is the will of God, that I should not lose even one of all those he has given me, but that I should raise them to eternal life at the Last Day. For it is my Father's will that everyone who sees his Son and believes on him should have eternal life—that I should raise him at the Last Day."

JOHN 6:35-40, TLB

I tell you the truth, he who believes has everlasting life. I am the bread of life. Your forefathers ate the manna in the desert, yet they died. But here is the bread that comes down from heaven, which a [woman] may eat and not die. I am the living bread that came down from heaven. If anyone eats of this bread, [she] will live forever. This bread is my flesh, which I will give for the life of the world.

JOHN 6:47-51

My sheep hear My voice, and I know them, and they follow Me. And I give them eternal life, and they shall never perish; neither shall anyone snatch them out of My hand. My Father, who has given them to Me, is greater than all; and no one is able to snatch them out of My Father's hand.

JOHN 10:27-29, NKJV

Let not your hearts be troubled; believe in God, believe also in me. In my Father's house are many rooms; if it were not so, would I have told you that I go to prepare a place for you? And when I go and prepare a place for you, I will come again and will take you to myself, that where I am you may be also.

JOHN 14:1-3, RSV

But now that you have been set free from sin and have become slaves to God, the benefit you reap leads to holiness, and the result is eternal life. For the wages of sin is death, but the gift of God is eternal life in Christ Jesus our Lord.

ROMANS 6:22-23

But I am telling you this strange and wonderful secret: we shall not all die, but we shall all be given new bodies! It will all happen in moment, in the twinkling of an eye, when the last trumpet is blown....

When this happens, then at last this Scripture will come true—"Death is swallowed up in victory." O death, where then your victory? Where then your sting? For sin—the sting that causes death—will all be gone; and the law, which reveals our sins, will no longer be our judge. How we thank God for all of this! It is he who makes us victorious through Jesus Christ our Lord!

1 CORINTHIANS 15:51-52,54-57, TLB

For our citizenship is in heaven, from which we also eagerly wait for the Savior, the Lord Jesus Christ, who will transform our lowly body that it may be conformed to His glorious body, according to the working by which He is able even to subdue all things to Himself.

PHILIPPIANS 3:20-21, NKJV

For the Lord himself will descend from heaven with a cry of command, with the archangel's call, and with the sound of the trumpet of God. And the dead in Christ will rise first; then we who are alive, who are left, shall be caught up together with them in the clouds to meet the Lord in the air; and so we shall always be with the Lord.

1 THESSALONIANS 4:16-17, RSV

Our Savior Jesus poured out new life so generously. God's gift has restored our relationship with him and given us back our lives. And there's more life to come—an eternity of life! You can count on this.

TITUS 3:6-8, MSG

Just as [woman] is destined to die once, and after that to face judgment, so Christ was sacrificed once to take away the sins of many people; and he will appear a second time, not to bear sin, but to bring salvation to those who are waiting for him.

HEBREWS 9:27-28

That is why they are here before the throne of God, serving him day and night in his temple. The one sitting on the throne will shelter them; they will never be hungry again, nor thirsty, and they will be fully protected from the scorching noontime heat. For the Lamb standing in front of the throne will feed them and be their Shepherd and lead them to the springs of the Water of Life. And God will wipe their tears away.

REVELATION 7:15-17, TLB

Then I saw a new heaven and a new earth, for the first
heaven and the first earth had passed away, and there was
no longer any sea. I saw the Holy City, the new Jerusalem,
coming down out of heaven from God, prepared as a
bride beautifully dressed for her husband. And I heard a
loud voice from the throne saying, "Now the dwelling of
God is with men, and he will live with them. They will be
his people, and God himself will be with them and be
their God. He will wipe every tear from their eyes. There
will be no more death or mourning or crying or pain, for
the old order of things has passed away."

REVELATION 21:1-4

I WILL USE YOU TO BLESS OTHERS

Turning the tide in our culture may seem like an impossible task,
but we are not alone in this challenge. *God* will turn the tide
through us. He simply asks us to submit our own lives to Him and
to be a witness to what His power and love can do. As more and
more women receive this revelation and share this wisdom with
others, the tide will eventually turn on its own.

—*Every Woman's Battle*

You are the light of the world. A city set on a hill cannot
be hid. Nor do [women] light a lamp and put it under a

bushel, but on a stand, and it gives light to all in the house. Let your light so shine before men [and women], that they may see your good works and give glory to your Father who is in heaven.

MATTHEW 5:14-16, RSV

And so if anyone breaks the least commandment, and teaches others to, [she] shall be the least in the Kingdom of Heaven. But those who teach God's laws and obey them shall be great in the Kingdom of Heaven.

MATTHEW 5:19, TLB

He who believes in Me, as the Scripture has said, out of his heart will flow rivers of living water.

JOHN 7:38, NKJV

But when the Holy Spirit has come upon you, you will receive power to testify about me with great effect, to the people in Jerusalem, throughout Judea, in Samaria, and to the ends of the earth, about my death and resurrection.

ACTS 1:8, TLB

What a wonderful God we have—he is the Father of our Lord Jesus Christ, the source of every mercy, and the one who so wonderfully comforts and strengthens us in our hardships and trials. And why does he do this? So that

when others are troubled, needing our sympathy and
encouragement, we can pass on to them this same help
and comfort God has given us. You can be sure that the
more we undergo sufferings for Christ, the more he will
shower us with his comfort and encouragement.

2 CORINTHIANS 1:3-5, TLB

For we are God's workmanship, created in Christ Jesus
to do good works, which God prepared in advance for us
to do.

EPHESIANS 2:10

Then we will no longer be infants, tossed back and forth
by the waves, and blown here and there by every wind of
teaching and by the cunning and craftiness of men in
their deceitful scheming. Instead, speaking the truth in
love, we will in all things grow up into him who is the
Head, that is, Christ. From him the whole body, joined
and held together by every supporting ligament, grows
and builds itself up in love, as each part does its work.

EPHESIANS 4:14-16

a final word

I pray that these passages of Scripture have whetted your appetite for even more of God's Word. Now that you've feasted on this collection of His promises, I'd like to leave you with a little sliver of dessert—pie crust!

Promises are like pie crusts—easily made, easily broken! Remember that saying? How well we learned about broken promises early in life, whether the lesson came from a friend, boyfriend, parent, or sibling. More than likely we've all experienced the unsettling surprise and bitter disappointment of a broken promise.

We've probably all broken at least one promise or two as well. Remember the promise you made to keep your girlfriend's secret to yourself, the secret you couldn't resist leaking to just one person (who also told one person, and so on)? Or remember the promise made to get up early to help your mother clean the house Saturday morning, but the covers felt too cozy not to sleep in? Or maybe you promised a boyfriend that you haven't spoken to in years that you would "love him forever!" You get the idea. Pie-crust promises. Easily made, easily broken.

But God simply *can't* break a promise He has made. He can't do anything that is contrary to His nature. He *is* truth and He cannot tell a lie. We can rejoice that each and every promise He has made is indeed ours to claim!

Consider this one last scripture:

> For no matter how many promises God has made, they are "Yes" in Christ. And so through him the "Amen" is spoken by us to the glory of God.
>
> 2 CORINTHIANS 1:20

Of all these verses that you have read in this promise book, there's not a single one that God will not carry through on. He *is* our friend, our Father, our Bridegroom. He *will* listen when we pray and draw near to us when we draw near to Him. He *will* protect you from the Enemy and help you control your fleshly desires. He *will* give you beauty for ashes and reveal His ways to you. He *will* reward you for your obedience. He *will* do *all* these things…and that, my friend, is a promise you can count on.

guys aren't the only ones fighting a battle for purity

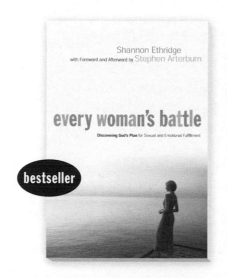

Women, like men, are fighting dangerous sexual battles. The only way you as a woman can survive the intense struggle for sexual integrity is by guarding not only your body, but also your mind and heart. From the coauthor of the Every Man series, Stephen Arterburn, and best-selling author Shannon Ethridge, *Every Woman's Battle* and *Every Young Woman's Battle* are designed to challenge and equip women of all ages to live sexually and emotionally pure lives.

Protect your sexual integrity and live your life to the fullest—without regrets.

Available in bookstores everywhere.

To learn more about WaterBrook Press and view
our catalog of products, log on to our Web site:
www.waterbrookpress.com